GHOST STORIES OF MANITOBA

GHOST STORIES OF MANITOBA

BARBARA SMITH

First printed in 1998 10 9 8 7 6 5 4 3
Printed in Canada

The Publisher: Lone Pine Publishing

#206, 10426-81 Avenue
Edmonton, AB T6E 1X5
Canada

202A 1110 Seymour Street
Vancouver, BC V6B 3N3
Canada

1901 Raymond Ave., SW, Suite C
Renton, WA 98055
USA

Lone Pine Publishing web site: http://www.lonepinepublishing.com

Canadian Cataloguing in Publication Data
Smith, Barbara, 1947–
Ghost stories of Manitoba

Includes bibliographical references.
ISBN 1-55105-180-X

1. Ghosts—Manitoba. 2. Legends—Manitoba. I. Title.
GR580.S6415 1998 398.2'09712705 C97-911021-1

Senior Editor: Nancy Foulds
Editor: Lee Craig
Production Management: David Dodge
Design, Layout and Production: Michelle Bynoe
Cover Design: Michelle Bynoe
Printing: Webcom Limited, Toronto, Ontario, Canada
Photography: The Liberal Party of Canada (p. 73); the Department of Archives & Special Collections, The University of Manitoba (p. 77, 80, 82, 155, 228); provided by Russ Mead (p. 83); the Provincial Archives of Manitoba (p. 17, 99, 103, 115, 121, 122, 182); Kat Morgan (p. 129); and Bonnie Robbins (p. 213).

The publisher gratefully acknowledges the support of the Department of Canadian Heritage.

Dedication

This book is dedicated to my friend Dr. Barrie Robinson, native Manitoban and former professor of sociology at The University of Manitoba and Brandon University.

For my grandsons and their peers—who will need forests as much as books—arrangements have been made to plant trees to compensate for those used in publishing this volume.

Contents

Acknowledgements

Many people have contributed to this book of Manitoba ghost stories. In compiling the stories I have counted on friends and relatives who have kept the project in mind as they went about their daily routines. Their support has been deeply appreciated but it is not surprising, because these are people I rely on for support in many aspects of my life. What has been an absolutely heartwarming surprise is the tremendous input I have received from total strangers. People I've never met and who had previously certainly never heard of me or my work have gone to an amazing amount of trouble to assist me. Often, the assistance they were offering was so unselfish that they didn't even leave me their names. To all of you anonymous contributors, I say a warm and grateful "thank you."

Others have been equally helpful and have left me their names. I would like to take this opportunity to extend a public "thank you" to several people. Paranormal writer and lecturer W. Ritchie Benedict, of Calgary, has to rank as the most tenacious researcher I have ever had the good fortune to meet. He got wind of my venture early on in its inception and from that moment he kept my search in the forefront of his mind as he went about his own investigations. The leads he supplied were numerous and valuable. During the early months of 1997, we had as many as three letters or packages flying back and forth between the two of us each week. Thank you, Ritchie, for sharing your time and skills to help me complete this book. Your unselfish diligence is deeply appreciated.

While researching for stories, I have learned to treasure librarians and archivists—their knowledge and willingness to help have consistently been invaluable. Even though some people in that capacity have only been anonymous voices across phone lines, I thank them sincerely for their friendly guidance and direction. Both Lynne Champagne, of the Provincial Archives of Manitoba, and Patricia Anderson, of The University of Manitoba Archives, went to a great deal of trouble to make sure I had everything I needed from their resources. Thank you to both of you.

Naomi Lakritz, a reporter for the *Winnipeg Sun,* unselfishly shared her experiences and accounts with me as did Winnipeg psychic Shelley O'Day. Betty Somers, of the Manitoba Historical Society, provided me with a lead that turned into one of my favourite stories in the collection (p. 55). British Columbia writer and researcher Nancy Bennett not only gave me permission to use three stories that she had collected, but actually sent them to me. Bonnie Robbins, of Brandon, sent along the White Horse legend (p. 212) and has kept in touch faithfully throughout the entire time the book was a work in progress. My most sincere thanks to all of you.

Introduction

Ghost Stories of Manitoba—a book of ghost stories from a province named to honour Manitou, a supernatural being. *What an ideal project,* I thought. *There should be a host of folklore phantoms here.* My intuition certainly proved to be correct, but in reality I doubt that the origin of the province's name was much of a determining factor. While the coincidence of the name was a decidedly nice touch for my particular project, credit for the numbers of ghost stories around Manitoba should, more properly, go to the province's colourful history and its diverse ethnic mix. Both have combined to leave a proud heritage and a population of friendly citizens who are happy to share their bit of that legacy.

A few of the stories in this book are rooted in the earliest history of European exploration. Other stories were still on-going even as my correspondents described their encounters with the Manitoba phantoms to me. Although some of these ghost stories are culturally based, I have, for the most part, avoided tapping the rich cache of aboriginal stories only because I do not feel qualified to attempt such a project. I hope someone else does write that book. I would love to read it.

The majority of the native peoples' stories are not the only ones I've chosen to leave out of this current work. People have sent me other intriguing tales that I've decided not to include. For instance, I have received stories of uncanny, and often lifesaving, premonitions, but whenever such a story did not directly include a ghost I've omitted it from the collection. Angels are another popular phenomenon and people have asked if I would include those sorts of stories. Like the native peoples' stories, I simply don't feel qualified to report on angel sightings or interventions.

Besides, I had to draw the line somewhere and so I chose to stay as true to the book's title as possible. Therefore, all the stories, save one, take place in Manitoba and include the presence of a spirit of some sort or another. In addition, all the chronicles in this book are believed by the people who have related the tales to me.

Having set those parameters, it would be most helpful if the reader and the writer could next agree on a definition for the word "ghost." Unfortunately, that consensus is not as easy to arrive at as one might first think. After having spent most of the last five years collecting ghost stories, I must confess that I'm still not much closer than I ever was to answering many of the questions that originally set me on my mission: What is a ghost? Why do some who have died return to this dimension while others seem to depart completely and forever? Why are some people more likely to be aware of a ghost's presence than others are? What causes one place to be haunted while another apparently remains a ghost-free zone? Those quandaries intrigue me as much today as they ever did.

Over the years a number of interesting theories have been presented to address those questions. Frederic Myers, author of *Human Personality and Its Survival of Bodily Death* (1903) and one of the founding members of the old and honourable Society for Psychical Research in England, suggested that a ghost is "an indication that some kind of force is being exercised after death" and that this force "is in some way connected with a person" now deceased. He further purported that ghosts are unaware of themselves and incapable of thought.

Most other explanations are variations of the one presented by Frederic Myers. "Leftover energy" (physical or emotional) is a term used to describe the phenomenon that is a ghost. The "psychic imprint" theory holds that the essence of a person has been somehow stamped on the environment in which that person lived. The deceased person's soul has effectively left its mark behind on the physical world. This "mark" can also be referred to as a "place memory" or a "residual haunting." The energy created by highly charged emotions from the past has been etched into the surroundings.

While reading this book or examining any of the literature available in the field, you might notice the frequency with which the word "energy" is used in discussions about ghosts and hauntings. It seems to be evident that spirits require energy to manifest themselves on our physical plane. Perhaps this is the reason radio stations and schools are frequently haunted, as are buildings near high voltage power lines. Even the energy created by the surging hormones of adolescence can draw spirits.

Another theory that attempts to explain the phenomenon holds that ghosts are disembodied souls (or energies or personalities or spirits) that are usually detectable only by our nearly atrophied "sixth sense." Rather than perceiving this otherworldly sensation with our familiar five senses, we notice reactions such as the hair on our arms or on the back of our neck standing on end, our skin tingling or simply the strange sensation that we are not alone or even that we are being watched.

Other students of the subject subscribe to the hypothesis that a ghost is a deceased person whose being either doesn't know he or she is dead or can't accept death because he or she feels obligated to complete unfinished business among the living.

Throughout all of these suppositions is the underlying question: Does a ghost originate with the living person who is experiencing the encounter or with the ghost itself? Perhaps that point is debatable, but because many people report seeing or sensing the same spirit either at the same time or at different times, the latter point appears closer to the truth. The event is certainly more objective than merely a figment of "the mind's eye."

The most striking of all the theses is that of "retrocognition"—being allowed to see or sense a piece of the past as it was actually lived. In this book, the story of "The Haunted Plains" (see p. 210) provides an example of retrocognition.

Another concept, that of "forerunners," or precognition, is almost the opposite of retrocognition. Forerunners are sightings that lead people to predict future events. Undeniably some ghosts, such as forerunners, have messages for us but others just seem to be continuing with their business, oblivious to the world of the living that surrounds them.

Despite this lack of agreement over what ghosts might be, their existence is attested to in all cultures and throughout history. My own experience collecting ghost stories has taught me one other widespread consistency—a paranormal encounter is a deeply moving experience. I have yet to have a story told to me in a flippant or even matter-of-fact way. Experiencing a ghost is clearly a profound occurrence in a person's life. Out of respect, I have agreed to protect a contributor's anonymity when he or she has requested I do so.

Encountering a ghost is an event that some people are much more likely to experience than others. I have heard the suggestion that some people are more tuned to the wavelength on which ghosts transmit. Although this attribute seems to be naturally occurring, it is also apparent that the ability can either be enhanced or diminished with practice.

Being haunted is not necessarily a permanent status for either a person or a place. Because a place was once haunted, does not mean that it always will be. Often, one of two things appears to happen: some ghosts seem to move on, perhaps satisfied with having accomplished a goal, or the energy that causes their existence eventually dissipates to a level where their presence is no longer strong enough to be felt by the living.

Conversely, other ghosts are incredibly tenacious. The ghosts of Roman soldiers are still occasionally spotted roaming the English countryside where they battled centuries ago. Such reports are the oldest I have ever discovered. I certainly have never heard of anyone being haunted by the ghost of a caveman.

If a place is haunted or if a ghost is present, predictable and distinguishable changes will usually be noticed. These changes could include a dramatic temperature drop. This sudden coldness could be very localized or encompass a larger area. There might be drafts or odours or noises—all of which seem, initially at least, to be sourceless.

To add even further confusion to a subject already filled with variables, the issue of semantics arises in the re-telling of these stories. There are few true synonyms in the English language, but I have chosen to use the following words interchangeably: spectre, spirit, entity, shade, presence, phantom, wraith and ghost. (I was informed once that the term "ghost" is an inherently insulting one. I hope that it's not so, because I certainly mean no offence by the term.)

While apparitions and poltergeists also fall under the broad definition of the word "ghost," they are not synonyms, because they have some additional qualities. An apparition is a visible presence; it has a discernible physical form. Although this definition tends to be the popular conception of a ghost, a sighting (that is, an apparition) is actually a statistical rarity.

A poltergeist is an equally rare type of spectral being that can be identified by its noisy and possibly violent behaviour. It will often move objects and can actually damage its surrounding physical environment. Poltergeists are strongly associated with people rather than places. They have been known to follow people for years, even through a succession of moves.

The ghost stories found in this book are not works of fiction. As a result, they tend to be more ragged than what we're used to. A fictional account of a haunting will have a nicely structured and highly satisfying presentation—a beginning, a middle and an end. The anecdotes recorded here refuse to be that tidy; they are often merely fragments, which can be somewhat frustrating in a world so fond of neatness. We like to have any loose ends bound up by the last sentence—it's much more gratifying that way. The reports presented here, however, are of real events and we all know that life as we live it is anything but neat and tidy. Because I consider myself merely a recorder of events, I have resisted the temptation to rework any of the stories to make them conform to an expected standard. To me, the missing parts of the puzzle are at least as provocative as the facts that have remained. My only concession to this premise has been to clarify a point and then I have restricted my input to either clearly attributed comments or to text surrounded by square brackets.

Because writers are traditionally cautioned to write only "what they know," I am frequently asked if I have ever seen a ghost. The short answer to that query is "no." I'm afraid that in the field of the paranormal I have very few first-hand qualifications. It is merely my love of social history, in addition to a lifelong fascination with the possibility that ghosts might exist, that has inspired me to write my books.

While writing and researching this book, I heard so many enticing hints of stories. Despite my best efforts, I wasn't always able to collect the information that the leads indicated was out there. The rumour I have heard several times that "the Legislative Building is haunted" is perhaps the most frustrating of the "big ones that got away." I searched for reports to validate what I'd heard. When I began to read the article that ran under the headline "Are Two Phantoms Really One" and found a reference to the Manitoba Legislative Building, I thought I'd finally nailed the story down. No such luck. The "phantom" referred to was certainly not from another dimension—he was a streaker. While the anecdote was amusing, it was hardly appropriate for inclusion in this book.

If anyone knows the story of the haunted halls of government, or, for that matter, any other Manitoba ghost story, I'd be delighted to hear from you. Please feel free to contact me through Lone Pine Publishing (see p. 4 for address).

For now, however, I hope you enjoy this collection of homegrown ghost stories. I wish you hours of eerie and thought-provoking reading—keep the lights on!

Chapter 1

HAUNTED HOUSES

The Old Geezer

The following story certainly supports the theory that children are more sensitive to the other realm than adults are.

Susan, a Winnipeg resident, explained that during the 1970s, when she was ten years old, her parents purchased a home in the north end of Winnipeg. It had been built in 1926 and so already had a lengthy history, unknown, of course, to Susan's family.

"Upon entering the house I immediately felt uneasy, verbalized dislike for the house and was told it would look differently after it was painted. While I was in bed the first night, I came to the conclusion that the house was haunted, twenty-nine years later we all know the house is haunted."

Susan's family gave the presence a name of sorts as many people with extraordinary companions do. When they didn't refer to him as "the man," it was "the old geezer." Susan knows her family had the gender correct for she actually saw the apparition.

"As a teenager I remember sitting in the living room late at night watching T.V. My parents' room is right off the living room so I sat on the floor in front of the T.V. with the volume low. All the lights in the house were out. Suddenly, I felt as if I were being watched. It was one of those moments when you feel those wee hairs at the back of your neck stand straight out. I turned quickly and there in the hall stood an old man."

Any ghostly sighting is an extraordinary experience, but the details Susan discerned make this report especially dramatic. "His image was made entirely of speckled and dispersed light. Clad in what I believed to be a hat and suit jacket length coat, he stood looking my way. Moments later, he moved from the hall into my bedroom!"

The youngster was understandably unnerved and remembers feeling angry that her parents had not listened more closely to her concerns when they were deciding whether to buy the house. Throughout her adolescence, Susan continued to be aware of the apparition's presence in the family home.

In 1981, after living on her own successfully for a number of years, Susan returned to live in her parents' home to complete her education and realize her dream of becoming a nurse.

Not long after she moved back into the house, the ghost recognized her return to his domain. Susan explained, "I returned home one afternoon just in time to make an important call. With about three minutes to spare I ran to my room, shut the door, sat on the bed, and picked up the phone. As I began to dial, the door [to the room] opened and then slammed shut. It did this repeatedly until the clock passed 5:00 p.m. and there was no point in completing the call. During the few minutes the door slamming occurred, I called out angrily, 'Tim, stop it!' thinking that my brother, eight years my junior, was playing a prank. The door was located no more than three feet from where I was sitting and I bolted up and through the door[way] to discover no one was there. I proceeded up the stairs and stood in front of the T.V., yelling and accusing Tim of making me miss a very important call.

"My father said, 'You don't know what you're talking about, he's been in your mother's room for the last half hour blow-drying his hair.'"

A quick glance into her parents' room confirmed the older man's words. That incident, however, marked the beginning of a series of events that the family will never forget.

Both Susan and her brother, then fifteen years of age, occupied bedrooms in the basement of the house. Teenaged boys often aren't too particular about housekeeping and Tim was no exception. Susan described her brother's small bedroom as usually being "a total disaster."

"One evening, with a lot of persuasion, he cleaned, polished and vacuumed his room. He had a set of weights which he stacked neatly in the corner of the room. With great pride, he showed me what he had done [and] soon after everyone retired. Shortly after 1:00 a.m., I was awakened by what I thought was an explosion. With horror my first thought was that the furnace blew [up]. It was located under the stairs and I feared Tim and I were trapped.

"I bolted out the door and turned on the light. The furnace was fine. I went up the stairs and checked my other brother's room and my parents' room. Everyone slept soundly. I went back to my room wondering what was going on."

Not knowing what else to do, Susan went back to bed, telling herself she'd been dreaming. Seconds later a pale and badly shaken Tim opened Susan's bedroom door. The boy swore softly under his breath when his sister asked him what was wrong.

"Didn't you hear that big noise?" he asked incredulously.

Susan assured Tim that she had. Before she could explain that she'd already checked the entire house and that all was well, the youngster motioned for her to come with him.

"We went to the door of his room, which now looked as if a tornado had gone through. Papers, clothing and furniture were everywhere. The set of weights was on his bed," Susan related.

She noticed her brother was rubbing his head. The lad explained, "My weights hit me on the head while I was sleeping."

"Tim was terrified and frankly, so was I. He slept on the foot of my bed for the rest of the night."

The next morning, the pair spoke to their mother about the incident. They pleaded with her to get a priest to visit. She refused, but perhaps later regretted it when the next night she was the target of "the old geezer's" explosive activity.

Susan's father was away on business that night and the rest of the family had gone to bed when they heard an explosion similar to the one of the night before. For the second night in a row, Susan raced upstairs to investigate the sound.

"My mother's door was open and she was sitting upright in bed, cursing up a storm. Her bedroom door had been thrown open with such extreme force that it had moved the dresser behind it," Susan remembered. She added, ironically, that for someone who didn't acknowledge the existence of the presence her mother certainly, "told something or someone off in no uncertain terms. My mother proceeded to say that she was paying the mortgage and that whoever he was should 'Go away and get the hell out of her house.'"

For a few minutes the frightened little group attempted to reassure one another before Susan's mother pulled rank and "commanded we all go to sleep." Not surprisingly, very little sleep was to be had in that once quiet household in the north end of Winnipeg. The experience, however, did force Susan's mother to admit that she, too, had seen the ghost.

Animals often act as though they see something that their owners don't and the family dog was no exception. "I cannot tell you the number of times she jumped off the bed barking at 'nothing.' Often awakened by this, I didn't know whether to curse at what I couldn't see or [to] smack … the dog. I often did both," Susan said.

The strain of living with a ghost can take its toll on a family. To retain at least some harmony, people often find humour in their bizarre circumstances. So it was with Susan's family. One afternoon, in typical teenaged brother fashion, Tim and his best friend Ricky sneaked into Susan's bedroom while she was out. Unaware that his friend's house had a resident ghost, the visitor stared in horror as the closet door in Susan's room began to open and close, apparently by itself.

"To this day Ricky will not go down into the basement," Susan added.

Despite the obvious drawbacks of living in a haunted house, the family stayed on. Not everyone has experienced the paranormal boarder. Neither Susan's father nor her older brother, Dan, has ever encountered anything untowards in the family's home.

Ten years ago Susan married a man whom she claims is "one of the world's biggest skeptics." Early last spring, Susan and her husband offered to help re-paint the inside of her parents' home.

"It was mid-afternoon and as I sanded the wall I got a very strange feeling. I turned to see the ghost standing not three feet behind my husband. I turned away quickly and when I looked back he was gone. I got a quick and strong case of the chills ... followed by a very bad case of the giggles. I told my husband 'he' was standing just behind him. My husband looked at me, shook his head and kept on painting."

Truly, some people are more closely attuned to the frequency phantoms are on. Despite the fact that Susan's husband painted through the "close encounter" with his in-laws' resident spook, not all of those who have married into this haunted family have been free of experiences.

In the intervening years Tim married, and at one point he and his wife, Audra, decided to move into the basement of Tim's parents' house. When Susan heard of their plans, she reminded them, "He's not going to like it."

"It appears that I was correct," Susan continued. "Mid-September, while in the recreation room, Audra met the man. She told us that he suddenly appeared and actually blocked out the sun, which came in the window. He then approached her and touched her arm."

Susan added, somewhat redundantly, "This was not a pleasant experience."

Despite all the activity throughout the years, the family has stayed on, sharing their home with an unpleasant and sometimes downright frightening ghost for thirty years.

"In ten months it will be our thirtieth anniversary in that house," Susan said. "It has truly become our family home albeit a family home with a little extra. The old man has scared us beyond disbelief yet made us laugh at times. He is definitely a part of our memories past, present and probably future."

The Waterford Ghost

Laurie Howard looks back fondly on the period of her life when she lived in a haunted house. And it's no wonder. Few associations, even with living people, are as heartwarming as Laurie's relationship was with the ghost in her house on Waterford Avenue.

"I enjoyed remembering about her and recounting our relationship," Laurie assured me.

It's fortunate that the story did turn out to be such a happy one because the first signs that Laurie had when she moved into the house in 1974 were not tremendously positive.

"I would wake up in the night sweating like a pig. My night clothes would be damp from perspiration and often I would be gasping for air."

Other times Laurie would wake up in the morning to find herself downstairs on the couch, unable to remember having moved from her bedroom.

"I found this so curious that I started looking for answers." This search must have been frustrating because Laurie soon surmised, "[T]here seemed to be no logical answer. The window was only a single pane and seemed to be draughty all around it. There was only one heating vent [in that room] and the temperature [in the room] was not individually controlled. So why did I feel like I was about to spontaneously combust every night in my sleep?" the young woman asked rhetorically.

She might never have suspected that her heating abnormalities had a paranormal origin, except that her belongings began moving about mysteriously.

"I was truly puzzled," she confessed. Little did she know that her confusion had barely begun.

"One day I was sitting on the mattress reading. I could actually feel the temperature rising in the room. I took off my sweatshirt and threw it on the table. While I was reading I could sense some movement. I looked up to see my sweatshirt hit the floor. The room was absolutely stifling. I got up and folded the shirt and put it right in the middle of the table," Laurie stressed. She had been willing to entertain the possibility that when she'd thrown the shirt on the table, it might have landed in such a way that it could have slipped off. "I went to the washroom and washed my face to cool down. When I went back into the bedroom, it was like walking into an oven, and there was my shirt, back on the floor."

By now the heat in Laurie's bedroom was so intense that it was making her feel ill. As Laurie expressed it, "This was a typical 'Peg winter day' … there was no reason for this draughty room to be so hot. The heat was not even coming through the register at this moment. I walked around the house and every room felt comfortable with a sweater on.

"What was going on?" Laurie wondered and added, "I wasn't scared, but I did feel something strange and I couldn't put my finger on it."

Laurie Howard was clearly a pragmatic young woman, for she set about trying to assure herself that there was a reasonable, physical explanation for at least some of her strange experiences.

"I went down to the basement and got the level out of the toolbox." She was hoping to prove to herself that her sweatshirt had slid off the table in her bedroom because the table top surface was uneven. Unfortunately for Laurie's peace of mind at the time, her experiment failed to prove her point. "When I placed [the level] on the table, the bubble floated dead centre. The table was level."

Under other circumstances, it might have pleased someone to discover that the house they were living in had no obvious sags and that their tables stood level. In this case, however, the normally good news did not bring her the reassurance that it could have and so she tested further.

"I got a marble and put it in various places on the table. Much to my chagrin, it would not roll off."

The scientific side of Laurie's mind simply couldn't accept any explanation other than the force of gravity being responsible for her sweatshirt twice falling onto the floor. Thoroughly intrigued by what was going on in her bedroom, Laurie went a step further by littering the top of the table from which her shirt had fallen, with "an ashtray, a bar of oatmeal soap, a glass of water and an impatiens plant."

Next, Laurie carefully noted the objects and their locations on the table before heading out to the store to buy a room thermometer.

"I practically raced up the stairs when I got home and there on the floor just outside the bathroom door was the bar of oatmeal soap."

Now, a woman of lesser courage would have looked for alternate accommodation but not Laurie.

"I felt spooked but not enough to turn and flee. I was strongly drawn to figure out what exactly was going on."

Laurie was interested to note that although the soap was the only item from the table that was no longer in her bedroom, all the other items had been moved. "[A]ll, that is, except the plant. I put my watch [back] in the ashtray and put the [ashtray] back where I had originally placed it. The book was on the floor and the glass of water was at the back of the table. I watered the plant with [the water from the glass] and put the glass back on the table. Once again, I could feel the room getting warmer by the minute. I ignored it for a while. I could feel my face getting flushed and my hands were getting clammy."

By now even logical Laurie had to admit something very out of the ordinary was going on. "I got up just as the empty glass hit the floor." This crash startled her enough that she decided it was time to check the recently purchased thermometer. "I [was] sure that it would be in the eighties, but it read sixty-five [degrees Fahrenheit]. When I turned back to the table, I noticed the ashtray was on its side and my watch was dumped out."

The calm, calculating side of Laurie's nature had finally reached its end. "Beads of perspiration were forming on my forehead. I didn't know what to do next. I couldn't tell people that I thought there was a ghost in my bedroom. They would think I was nuts," Laurie realized. "What would it prove anyway?"

Little changed for Laurie for a time and slowly she began to accept that she'd likely never find a physical cause for her bizarre living conditions. She continued to wake up in her living room when she'd gone to sleep in her bedroom and things that she placed on the table in her bedroom continued to be moved about, with one exception—the impatiens plant.

"It was thriving and its position never changed. I never moved it either, almost out of respect for whomever it was that I seemed to be annoying."

After a while Laurie and her invisible, but mischievous roommate, began to co-habit reasonably peacefully. By the time winter was finally over and spring had arrived, the woman decided to treat herself to a holiday. After making arrangements to have a friend pick up her mail while she was gone, Laurie left on vacation.

"I didn't leave the key because I didn't think there was any need to. I had shut the water off and everything," she explained.

At some point during her time away, Laurie suddenly remembered the impatiens plant. It was sure to die from neglect during her absence.

"I felt bad, like I had let her down." As though she was responding to the sudden use of gender in her description of the ghostly presence, Laurie added, "The ghost had now become a woman in my mind and had somehow worked her way into my heart."

Now this comment is especially interesting because Laurie had no way of knowing anything about the former owner of the house. She was only sub-letting the place from friends. Even so, however, it was obvious that long ago someone had lovingly cared for the grounds around the house.

"The overgrown remains of flower and vegetable gardens were barely discernible now, but at one time they were probably the pride and joy of a dedicated gardener. Wildflowers from stray seeds poked out of cracks in the driveway and foundation. The trees attested to the age of their surroundings and lent, not only shade, but an aura of peace and tranquillity."

Laurie also added that the house no longer compared well with its neighbours.

"The house stood out from all the others on the block as it was dilapidated."

Presuming the ghost was the former owner of the house and someone who'd kept the place up, Laurie commented that she "felt sorry for" the ghost and therefore terribly guilty that the impatiens plant—the one positive connection she had to the spirit of the former owner—would have died because of Laurie's own lack of forethought.

The young woman returned from vacation expecting the worst. As she explained, "... anyone who has ever had an impatiens plant would know that they need lots of water and tending, so when I returned home you could imagine my surprise when I saw the healthiest-looking plant in my entire life." Laurie knew immediately that something out of the ordinary had not only kept the plant alive but actually caused it to flourish.

"This was not physically possible and as I looked at [the plant] I had tears streaming down my cheeks and I was laughing out loud. The plant was overflowing its container and was covered in beautiful, pink blossoms," Laurie said. "I stuck my finger into the soil and it was bone dry."

By way of thanking her invisible horticulturist, Laurie set to work in the yard.

"I spent the next week in the backyard restoring the gardens. I planted some vegetables and put in numerous flats of bedding plants. I transplanted the impatiens plant into a hanging basket and hung it in a tree that could easily be seen from the bedroom window. I left a small slip [of the plant] out and planted [the slip] in a small pot and put it back on the table in the bedroom."

Within hours Laurie's kind attention to the property was rewarded.

"That night I awoke and felt a presence in the room. The room was not hot for a change. I was actually comfortable." Having wakened up so many nights from the intense heat in the room and feeling only a normal air temperature now, Laurie wondered what had wakened her out of a sound sleep.

"Then I saw her. She was very old with white hair wrapped into a neat bun. She had on a very plain black dress with a flower-printed apron over it. She was looking out the window and smiling. As fast as the apparition had appeared, she faded and disappeared. I was sitting bolt upright and I had tears in my eyes. Her smiling face had deeply touched my heart."

That instance created a definite bond between the home's current occupant and, presumably, a former one that lasted happily until the day Laurie moved out.

Some People Are More Haunted than Others

Occasionally, the way a ghost story reaches me is almost as intriguing as the story itself. The following tale fits securely into that category. W. Ritchie Benedict, a paranormal researcher in Calgary, Alberta, was among the many who were aware of my hunt for Manitoba ghost stories. When he spotted an appropriate article in the British magazine *Phoenix,* he sent it along to me. Not content with merely re-reporting this terrific story, I wrote to Alan

Baker, editor of the *Phoenix*, asking for more information. Just a few weeks later, two envelopes arrived in the mail for me. The larger of the two was from the United Kingdom and inside I discovered additional issues of Baker's magazine, both containing reports of hauntings in Manitoba and both written by a woman named Nancy Bennett. While still basking in the excitement of that coup, I noticed the second envelope had come from Victoria, British Columbia—more specifically from Nancy Bennett of that beautiful western capital. She wanted to let me know that Alan Baker had contacted her regarding my inquiry and that she was most anxious to help in any way she could.

And so, with my thanks to Mr. Benedict, Mr. Baker and especially to Nancy Bennett who kindly agreed to let me use the stories, here is a series of Manitoba ghost stories, all sharing a central character—a woman named Alana.

Nancy Bennett began by explaining what all of us who collect anecdotes about phantoms soon discover: some people are more likely to have an experience with a presence than others are. Certain people share the same "wavelength" as spirits and therefore receive their messages much more readily than others. This ability seems to be naturally occurring, but from all I've been told it would appear that you can either hone or suppress the talent, depending on your interest and comfort level.

For Alana, it was evident right from childhood that she was one of those people who possess an inherent awareness of the spirit world. She shared the ability with her mother who was also able to see and sense spirits. Alana's first remembered experience occurred when she was less than ten years of age. She had travelled, with her family, some distance to visit friends. The length of the journey was such that the visiting family was invited to spend the night with its hosts.

Alana and her brother were exhausted from the trip and so were put to bed early in adjoining bedrooms. The children fell asleep quickly. Both children would probably have slept right through the night, but were jolted awake by the sudden sensation that they were not alone in their rooms. Alana opened her eyes to gaze upon a gleaming white form. The apparition wore a bridal gown that glowed and seemed to float about the ethereal body that wore it.

Alana was so fascinated by the surreal dress that it took her a moment to realize there was something even more distressing about the presence in her room. The "bride" was headless. The little girl ran from the room in search of her brother. She found the lad in the hall. He was heading for the comfort of her bedroom because he was equally as frightened by something he'd seen: a disembodied woman's head floating about his temporary bedroom.

As the two children huddled together and exchanged their incredible stories, they both calmed considerably and were able to report the details of their sightings to one another. The head that the little boy saw must have belonged to the ghostly body that had visited Alana, for he declared that it had been wearing a white veil.

Little did Alana know then that the headless apparition would prove to be merely the first in a lifetime dotted with paranormal observations.

When the family moved into a home on McGregor Street in Winnipeg, Alana reported she felt very ill at ease in the house. They'd only lived there a short time when her mother began to see an image, that of a man wearing a red and black jacket. The apparition, which was crouched in a corner near the staircase to the basement, exuded such overwhelming sadness that it soon began to affect the older woman. She became convinced that the man whose spirit peered out at her from beyond had come to an unnatural end, in this house.

The woman began to look for clues that would substantiate her claim. She searched the attic of the house and was rewarded almost immediately. For there, in the dust, lay what remained of a red and black jacket. It was old and torn but still distinctive enough that the woman recognized it as being the jacket the ghost wore. Closer examination revealed a definite hole in the material, a hole that was surrounded by a blood-like stain.

The apparition's appearances increased dramatically after the jacket was found and so Alana's mother widened her search to include the home's unfinished basement. The area was considerably less than appealing, one the family had only used for storage. The cellar floor was bare earth and extended into a crawl space that had been blocked by barrels.

Taking Alana with her, the determined mother made her way into the previously barricaded space. The moment their eyes adjusted to the darkness, mother and daughter saw a sight they'll never forget—two mounds of earth.

"... They were the shape of graves," Alana attested simply.

Too frightened to continue their search, the two left their discovery for Alana's skeptical sister to investigate further. Laughing at her mother's and sister's fear, the youngster crept through the passage.

Initially, this second daughter must have thought she'd made a terrific find—the only article she unearthed from one of the mounds appeared to be a piece of gold. She happily showed it to her father who immediately dashed the child's hopes by declaring the nugget to be a worthless chunk of "fool's gold."

Even though no one in Alana's family was anxious to move again, they'd all had more than enough of life in a haunted house. While making the necessary arrangements and waiting to move, they made a point of avoiding the eerie basement. They moved from the haunted house without ever having investigated the second mound of dirt in the basement.

Whatever they might have unearthed there could have explained why the house was haunted. Today, we're left to wonder: Was a body buried there? Did someone get away with murder? Is the house still standing? Has the basement been fully excavated? Is the old place on McGregor Street still haunted or has the tormented soul finally found eternal peace?

Years passed, and Alana met the man she would eventually marry. While on a date, the couple drove to a nearby lake. All the locals, Alana and her friend included, were aware that there was an enduring legend associated with the area around this particular lake. It was said that some years ago a couple decided to indulge themselves in a relaxing holiday and rented a cabin by the lake. One evening the wife wanted to go for a walk but could not convince her husband to join her. His decision turned out to have been a tragic one for he never saw his wife alive again.

When the woman didn't return within what her husband thought was a reasonable length of time, he set out to look for her. She hadn't gotten far. Someone must have been watching the cabin and, as soon as she was a distance from the safety of the little dwelling, had raped and murdered her. The husband, apparently completely overcome with grief, killed himself by walking purposefully into the lake.

Since that day, it was said, on the anniversary of the couple's death, their apparitions could be seen. Over the years watching for the paranormal activity has become a popular pastime, especially with the young people in the nearby community. The reports were all the same and quite specific: "… Lights moved slowly from one room [of the cabin] into another, as if someone were carrying a candle. Shadows of two people could sometimes be seen."

Well, all of that might have been enough to have sparked interest in the thrill-seeking teens but Alana was different. She understood the essence of an actual sighting, because of her childhood experiences. As Nancy Bennett put it, "[Alana] was not about to be fooled by the charade."

Feeling she'd had her fill of adolescent histrionics, Alana suggested to her boyfriend that they drive back to town. And that's when they saw it—the sight neither can ever forget.

"Up along the treeline, a man and a woman were walking hand in hand. They were stepping on air as they went along the forest top, walking silently. The night, which had been alive with sounds, was suddenly plunged in a vacuous silence," Alana had recounted to Nancy Bennett. "[Alana] had had enough; she turned and hightailed it back to the car."

Neither the young woman nor her husband-to-be ever visited the area again. They married not long afterwards and, as planned, began a family almost immediately.

As with many newlyweds, finances were a problem. Their furnishings were decidedly sparse so when an acquaintance offered to give them a chair for their living room they were happy to accept the gift. At the time, of course, they had no way of knowing that this particular gift brought along more than what was always visible.

As any woman who has ever been in the latter stages of pregnancy can attest, sleeping through the night is not a luxury available during the weeks immediately prior to giving birth. Alana was no exception. One night during a trip to the washroom, the woman was aghast to see a man, dressed only in a well-worn housecoat, sitting on the newly received living room chair. The apparition might have been as surprised to see Alana as she was to see him, for he stared intently at her. Alana's reaction was considerably louder than that. She screamed. The man shook his head in disapproval before fading from sight.

The sightings of the man in the chair continued until Alana could not take the strain any longer. She made plans to give the chair away, reasoning that if the chair was not in the house, the house would not be haunted.

Alana's mother, who'd always admired the chair, offered to take it. She thought it would look nice in her other daughter's bedroom. Well, it might have looked very nice, but as soon as the chair was placed in her room, Alana's sister began to have nightmares. They were very specific nightmares, where she saw the image of a man in a housecoat sitting on the chair. After each dream, she would waken with a start and for just a second, actually see the same image that had unnerved her sister so.

Desperate for peace, the family disposed of the chair. That, thankfully, put a stop to the terrifying dreams and the sightings. It does not, however, explain where the spirit of the man could be now.

Shared Accommodation

When I'm asked, "How do you go about collecting ghost stories?" I never quite know how to reply. Often, people have had ghost stories in their family heritage for years and are only too happy to share them with me, for others to enjoy. Archival newspapers are another cache. Today, paranormal events are not often reported in our daily newspapers but years ago supernatural occurrences might well have made the front page; those stories were obviously extremely easy to locate. Simply talking to people, letting them know about my project, was another, occasionally successful, research method and the method by which I came to hear the following intriguing story.

After enjoying a twenty-minute conversation with a journalist in Thompson, I came away not only with the information I'd been after initially but also with a lead on a haunted house story—in a town situated in the southeast of the province, many miles from Thompson.

When I contacted the woman who'd owned the house, she agreed to share her story for publication in the book only on a promise of complete anonymity. This haunted house story was far too good to miss so I readily agreed to her request. The name of the town has purposely been omitted and the woman I spoke with shall be identified only as "Shirley."

Shirley had sold the property and gone on to new challenges. She was relating events that had occurred in a place that now belongs to someone else and so was legitimately reluctant to make any comments that might affect that person's life. Besides, she added hopefully, the house might well have become phantom-free by now.

From the cautious way Shirley couched her phrases, it seemed that she was trying very hard to be a skeptic in the face of what amounted to almost certain proof of the existence of spirits.

"We weren't the only ones who sensed it. People would come to visit us and they'd say, 'I'm not going into that room,'" she began. "After a while you get so you're spooking yourself crazy."

Having set her disclaimers as firmly in place as she could, Shirley began to relate the history of her family's involvement with the haunted house.

"We bought the place in September 1994, but didn't move in until the following April," she explained. This interval gave the family time to make the necessary renovations to the house, and it also gave Shirley a chance to research the home's unusual history.

It seems a young couple had bought the place during the Depression in the 1930s. It's safe to assume from the events as they unfolded that having the house and raising a family there were cherished dreams for these people. Sadly, they were only able to realize one of those dreams. When the woman became pregnant, they were ecstatic. They immediately set about lovingly preparing one of the upstairs rooms as a nursery. When the child was born they were overjoyed, but their happiness was short lived. The baby died in infancy.

Unable to accept the tragedy, the couple preserved the baby's room exactly as it had been before the child's death. The result was a permanent, eerie illusion not only that the child was still alive but, impossibly, perpetually an infant.

It is not known whether the tragedy caused the woman to become a recluse or whether she'd always been an extremely introverted person. From today's perspective it really doesn't make any difference, it is only important to note Shirley's explanation that from then on, "the house was her life."

"She had the place set up 'just so.' She cleaned it from top to bottom—that was her domain. She had the ladies in for bridge occasionally but that was about all. She rarely went out. Her husband was usually in the basement with his dog," Shirley said.

The couple retained this strictly regimented and self-sufficient order until his death more than forty years later. Shortly afterwards, although she was loathe to leave her beloved home, the widow moved to a nursing home. Evidently, the only way she could accept this removal was to think of it as a temporary accommodation to circumstances and she made sure everyone at the nursing home was very clear about that, too.

"She told all the ladies that looked after her in the nursing home that she was definitely going home," Shirley explained.

Given this conviction, it was only reasonable that she wouldn't think of selling her home. What became somewhat unreasonable were the lengths to which the woman went to support her fantasy. She actually paid people to keep the house clean, tidy and stocked with provisions. This poignant and expensive fabrication went on until the woman's death more than ten years later. The house was sold by the woman's estate.

"There were two young couples who lived there before we bought it. The couple we bought it from had similar experiences [to ours]," Shirley told me.

Not long after they settled in, Shirley and her family realized they were not alone. It seemed that the elderly couple had never really left. Even more interesting was that the territorial division the pair had worked out for themselves in life was clearly continuing on well after their deaths.

Shirley first sensed the woman's presence when she was working in an upstairs room, the room that had formerly been the museum-like nursery. Seemingly, the previous owner was curious about what was now happening in the room that had once been a monument to her grief.

Shirley said that realizing what she was dealing with made living and working in and around a haunted house somewhat less stressful.

"We took to talking to her—asking if what we were doing with the place was all right with her. She seemed to approve and yet the whole time we were there it was a real struggle," Shirley recalled, her voice trailing off as she added, "She was so fastidious."

Night-time was a particular challenge for the whole family.

"It was very noisy at night. There were unexplainable noises. Some nights the noises woke the family up. [The next morning] the kids would say, 'Did you hear the scratching in the middle of the night last night?' [Other nights] I would wake up and sit up and look around for the people making the noise but, of course, no one was ever there. Sometimes you'd hear something that sounded like plastic flapping in the wind but it was inside,"

Shirley explained before summarizing the disturbances as "just a lot of goings on."

Family members were not the only ones who were aware of the presences in the house.

"People liked to go upstairs in the house and see how everything was decorated. The beds would be all made up but often when there hadn't been anyone up there, there'd be impressions on the covers as though someone had been sitting on them. In the basement the feeling was different," Shirley continued. "I had worked myself into being spooked about going down there. You know, there's that last load of laundry you should do late at night but often I'd look down there and just couldn't bring myself to go down. Then one night I had a dream about him [the former owner]. I dreamed that I went into the basement and he was standing there beside a steam boiler but that he was a young man. I chatted with him and after that I felt better about going into the basement. If he was there, I knew he was friendly."

Shirley had commented to my contact in Thompson that she'd heard the husband had been a "happy-go-lucky" type of person and this attitude was then reflected in the atmosphere in the basement. Shirley explained that after having experienced the reassuring dream, the basement "became [a] warm and dark and comfortable and friendly" area of the house. This perception was a definite contrast to the previous feeling of "being clucked at" while she was on other floors.

Although Shirley attested that she had eventually "reached an accommodation with the ghosts," her family decided to move on. She hasn't heard whether or not the new owners have had any unusual experiences, but readily admits that her desire to protect their identity might be somewhat futile. By now, they might be all too aware that they are living in a haunted house.

The Ghosts Are Gone Now

It was the summer of 1979 and the Chandler family excitedly prepared to move into their newly purchased home in Brandon's east end. At the time they considered themselves fortunate, for it was a particularly attractive house and one that had come on the market quite unexpectedly. The vendors had only recently bought the house and had hoped to enjoy living in it for a very long time. Unfortunately, they'd no sooner moved in than the husband's employer saw the need to transfer him to another city. The family had no choice but to list the house for sale and it was then that the Chandlers spotted the "For Sale" sign.

Thrilled with having made their very first real-estate investment, Mr. and Mrs. Chandler, along with their two teenaged daughters, Amy and Brett, moved into their "quaint, Tudor-style" home. Not long after, both youngsters reported hearing footsteps in the kitchen and on the back stairs. Their parents didn't take the comments too seriously. After all, no one could have a more vivid imagination than a teenaged girl, unless, of course, it was two teenaged girls, especially ones who had recently been uprooted with a family move.

But active imaginations were not the only thing Amy and Brett had in common with others of their age and gender; they were also endlessly curious. The two girls wanted to discover the world they saw all around them, as well as the world that was beyond their sight. Towards this end, the sisters decided it would be fun to hold a seance.

Their attempt to contact the world beyond was a success if judged solely by the fact that they obviously did make contact with the spirit world. A woman who knows the family, however, stated flatly, "The seance turned out to be the worst thing they could have done." A family member who has asked not to be identified explained, "All it did was to encourage the paranormal activity in the house."

The phantom footsteps now occurred regularly, at predictable times. Even though neither Amy nor Brett was concerned that the ghost would harm them in any way, living in a haunted house was beginning to take its toll on both of them. They became uncomfortable about going home after school and when they did they would stay in the basement under the guise of watching television—with the volume turned way up to drown out the sounds of the footsteps.

Despite their daughters' admittedly uncharacteristic behaviour, neither Mr. nor Mrs. Chandler had yet begun to take the youngsters' concerns seriously. Mr. Chandler, however, was effectively stripped of his complacency one Saturday afternoon when he was alone in the house. As the man sat at his dining room table, he clearly heard footsteps pass directly behind him. Pleased to realize that this sound must have meant his family had come back, he turned around to greet them.

He was alone.

That was enough to convince him that neither Amy nor Brett had been victims of over-active imaginations but that there was something very strange going on in their house. He began to research the history of the house before the previous owner had bought it. He discovered that the house his family now called "home" had been owned for many years by a woman who had recently been killed in a car accident. Could this woman's spirit be the source of the apparently sourceless footsteps? Perhaps she had died so suddenly that her soul had not been able to grasp the fact that she was dead. If this were the case, then habit and a search for comfort might have caused her soul to return to this house where she'd happily lived for so long.

Now that Mrs. Chandler was the only member of the family not to have had a direct encounter with the spirit, it was easier for Amy and Brett to discuss their experiences and feelings connected with living in a haunted house. They explained that their amateur seance had possibly given them more than they had bargained for. They suspected that it had unleashed a second presence into the house—a presence that had not left when the ill-fated seance ended.

This spirit, which was considerably more unsettling than the original one, was never identified but it, too, was attracted to the staircase in the house. Mr. Chandler and his daughters would frequently hear the sound of pebbles falling down the stairs and yet no pebbles were ever found. The three family members might have been able to put up with this stunt, but this ghost's affinity for doorknobs was more than they could endure.

"It ... liked to turn door handles, but never opened any of the doors," recalled a family friend who asked not to be identified.

Brett, the elder of the two teenagers, admitted, "It's quite unnerving to watch a doorknob turn and know there isn't anybody on the other side."

The situation continued for months until Mrs. Chandler, the only member of the household not to have experienced the spirits, finally suggested that her daughters "have a talk with the spirits. Tell them that we are sorry they are dead and that we are sorry we disturbed them but that they should leave." Amy, especially, thought her mother's advice was good and she followed through with it.

The family friend with whom the Chandlers shared their story commented, "Remarkably, the haunting soon ceased." The presences and phantom sounds that haunted three-quarters of a family for nearly a year had been laid to rest.

The Cold House

The following story occurred more than forty years ago in a house that was then located in the Ellice and Burnell area of Winnipeg. The family who had this experience asked specifically that its identity be concealed. As you read through the story I'm sure you will understand both why the folks involved requested anonymity and why I gladly abided by that request. The names that follow are pseudonyms.

Just after World War II, the Bakkers moved to Winnipeg, choosing an older house in which to make their home. They were of German descent and spoke little English. As a result, the family members were very much outsiders in the community. Their isolation makes their experiences even more poignant.

The first thing the family noticed in its "new" house was that it was constantly cold. At first no one connected this inconvenience with what was to follow—the pitter-patter of child-like footsteps at times when there was no rational explanation for such sounds. Just as they grew somewhat used to those sounds, they began hearing the distinct sound of giggling.

Some weeks later the children of the household began to complain that their sleep was being interrupted by an image of a small girl. As their mother was a pragmatic sort who had more than enough in her life to cope with, she did not take her youngsters' complaints too seriously—at first.

Like many parents, Mrs. Bakker would check on each of her children before she retired to bed herself. And that's when she first saw the apparition—a blonde girl surrounded by a hazy, blue aura. After that first sighting, she frequently had the sense that someone was following her as she went on her rounds, checking on her sleeping children.

The children's mother became concerned about living in a haunted house, but the family's financial resources were very limited and so, therefore, were its options. Rather than consider moving, the woman decided to address the problem—the ghost, that is—directly. In her native language she asked the ghost what it wanted and why it kept following her. The ghost answered in the Bakker's native language; she explained that she was cold.

Mrs. Bakker must have determined that the spirit meant no harm, for the family lived on in the haunted house for a period of time. Just before they were planning to move, the woman made a horrifying discovery. There, hidden in the basement, wrapped in brown paper, was a skull—a child's skull—with some of its blonde hair still attached. Panicking at the implications of her discovery, the woman showed it only to her husband. Together, they determined the best thing to do was to secretly dispose of the skull. They secured the tragic find in an old oil drum and immediately drove it to an out-of-town dump.

Anyone who would condemn the couple's actions as heartless and clearly illegal need only to recall that these people were immigrants of German descent during post-war days. Anti-German sentiment still ran high and as newcomers who did not fully understand the culture around them, they were motivated solely by fear.

As planned, the family moved on, adjusted well to its new country and became productive, happy citizens. We can only hope that the pathetic little apparition that haunted their first house in Canada has also moved on and become adjusted to her current status—in the "great beyond."

Ghost in the Window

Early in the summer of 1993, Robin Smyth and her boyfriend Paul drove across the entire breadth of Canada. They had both been students at the University of Victoria and were feeling the need to get away and experience life in different areas of the country.

With two drivers and long summer days, they were able to make good time. Being students, they were on an impossibly tight budget and had been sleeping in the car throughout the journey. One evening, just west of Falcon Lake, Manitoba, the pair decided it was time to stop for the night. They spotted a driveway leading from the highway and turned onto it in search of a safe place to spend the night.

"As soon as we turned off the highway, I had the distinct feeling that I didn't want to be there. I told Paul, 'Let's go somewhere else, I don't like it here,'" Robin recalled. But the young man was insistent. He had been doing most of the driving that day and the kilometres had taken their toll. Besides, Robin's discomfort aside, it looked as though the pair of travellers had happened upon an almost ideal, impromptu campsite.

"The driveway led to a deserted farm. It clearly had been a working farm but equally clearly it had recently been abandoned," Robin said.

To walk off the long hours spent sitting in the car, the two walked around, investigating the abandoned property for a while.

"We wandered all around the barns and the barnyard before approaching the farmhouse. We looked through the house. It was completely empty, except one chair in the living room facing out the picture window. I thought at the time it looked as though someone could have been sitting there saying good-bye to the place."

By now, Robin's feelings of discomfort were more than she could bear and it was her turn to be insistent. "We're not staying here tonight," she declared flatly.

Seeing there was little point in arguing, Paul walked with his increasingly upset girlfriend back to the car. As tired as he was, he knew Robin well enough to recognize the tone in her voice. They would have to find another spot to spend the night. As he backed the car up to turn it around, just for a second Paul's headlights illuminated the front window of the empty house—except that now it wasn't empty. A man, wearing a hat, stood staring out of the window, watching the young couple leave. Not wanting to make any further comments, Robin said nothing about what she saw. Paul, however, now realized what had made his girlfriend so uncomfortable for he saw the man as clearly as she did.

"Did you see that?" the young man exclaimed in shock. "That was a ghost!"

Robin nodded in agreement.

How did the two know they'd actually seen a ghost and not just a fellow traveller who'd beaten them to an ideal location for a free night's accommodation? It's simple. The man they saw at the window was ever-so-slightly see-through!

A Glimpse at the Past

Paranormal experts have varying opinions about why ghosts exist and even what they are. One theory is that of "retrocognition"—seeing or sensing the past. For reasons not yet understood, some of us are occasionally treated to a first-hand glimpse at history by experiencing retrocognition. A portion of the following story from Winnipeg's north side demonstrates this phenomenon well.

Donna had always been skeptical about the existence of ghosts, but evidence of a presence in her north-end home began almost immediately after she moved into it in 1987.

"I've heard heavy-set footsteps going down the stairs and female footsteps in high-heel shoes." But those intrusions were only the beginning.

"I had daily occurrences—cupboards would slam, lights would flicker, I'd hear voices call my name. I'd lie in the tub and hear 'Psst, psst' around me," Donna explained to *Winnipeg Sun* reporter Naomi Lakritz.

Although Donna was quickly becoming a believer, she was evidently not one to scare easily for she continued to live in what was quite obviously a haunted house. It wasn't until an incident one afternoon in 1992 that she began to become concerned. Donna was resting in an upstairs bedroom, reading a book when she noted a shadow at the end of the bed. Possibly wondering if someone was in her house, she made her way downstairs to investigate.

"My whole living room looked different," she stated simply, before elaborating. "I saw a bed with a girl lying in it."

Donna had just experienced retrocognition. The details of the vision from the past were clear. The apparition had shoulder-length dark hair, which was parted in the middle. Only the girl's head was exposed. The rest of her body was covered with a sheet and a blanket.

"I knew the girl wasn't sleeping. I knew she was dead."

Donna's gift of hindsight was only fleeting.

"I saw it in the bat of an eye and then it was gone," she recalled.

It was only after that sighting that Donna decided it was time to investigate. She began the process by contacting Winnipeg's well-known ghost-hunter, Roy Bauer. Bauer decided to check into the home's past. He contacted a previous owner who informed him that many years before she and her husband had lost their fifteen-year-old daughter, Dee Dee, to a terminal illness when they had lived in the house.

The child's mother was, by now, elderly and understandably upset by the possibility that someone outside her own family had been witness to something so intimate as a vision of her beloved daughter. The woman remarked that if the girl's spirit were to return, surely she would appear to her own mother, not to a complete stranger.

That argument, of course, depends entirely on the premise that an apparition manifests voluntarily, under its own initiative. In this particular instance there is absolutely no proof of that. Dee Dee's appearance would seem, instead, to have been a "psychic imprint" of sorts. This theory holds that the essence of a person somehow becomes stamped on the environment in which that person lived, and in this case, died. Dee Dee's soul, it would seem, had effectively left an imprint on the physical world.

Despite her hesitancy in accepting Donna's story, Dee Dee's mother did inquire as to whether Donna had ever heard the sounds of tapping shoes. Before she'd become ill, the teenager loved to tap dance. Donna, of course, immediately thought of the sounds she'd heard that sounded like someone walking in high-heel shoes.

None of this information, however, shed any light on the "heavy-set footsteps going down the stairs." After a little gentle probing, it was determined that Dee Dee's mother, now a widow, had been married to a large man who had worked for the railway. Because of the nature of his duties, the man was required to wear work boots. Now Donna knew why she heard the more forceful footfalls as well.

Feeling that she had identified the spirits with whom she shared her house, Donna thought it was best for both her and the spirits if she were to free them from what was now *her* home.

"I think a spirit can get locked in somewhere on a kind of plane," she asserted. Whatever method Donna used to release the entities must have been successful. She has since happily reported that things are now "all quiet on the homefront."

Not a Normal House

"It was definitely not a normal house," Eva Pip stated with conviction. By the time she'd explained some of the events that had occurred in the seemingly ordinary house on Manitoba Avenue in Winnipeg's north end, it was evident that her assessment was correct.

Eva's father purchased the home for his young family in 1950. He had intended the new piece of real estate to be a pleasant surprise for his wife and daughter, but he was sadly mistaken. His wife's reaction was immediate and far from positive.

"[S]he broke down in tears. The house seemed very unpleasant and depressing for her," Eva recalled before describing the physical appearance of the house. "It had been built in 1907. It was a storey and a half of old, unpainted, grey brick with a screened verandah at the front. The foundation was made of large blocks of stone mortared together."

Admittedly, not an attractive-sounding house, but surely not one so repellent as to reduce a grown woman to tears. Other factors must have been, and were, at work here—factors that Eva clearly remembered, despite the fact that she was only three years old at the time she first set foot in the house on Manitoba Avenue.

"My parents were looking around downstairs. I crawled up the stairs to the gloomy second floor. There was a closet opposite the head of the stairs. As soon as I reached the top and stood before the door of the closet, a feeling of great terror suddenly overwhelmed me," Eva explained. "I wanted to escape very badly, but was unable to get back down the stairs again. For some reason my limbs were paralyzed and I was unable to cry out for help. Eventually, my mother rescued me."

Despite this less-than-joyous introduction to their newly purchased property, the family soon moved in. That move marked the beginning of nearly twenty-five years of terror for Eva.

"[L]iterally hundreds of strange phenomena occurred there. Almost daily there were the sounds of footsteps, particularly in the entrance hallway at the base of the stairs."

The footfalls then proceeded up the stairs towards the closet at the top, where Eva had initially been held captive by some unseen force.

"Each stair would creak in succession as though someone were ascending or descending, even though there was nothing visible to the eye. Sometimes when I looked up the stairs, the closet door would slowly open by itself."

The sounds of footfalls weren't restricted to the stairs nor was Eva the only one to be aware of them. The rest of the family as well as visitors would often hear sounds made seemingly by no living person.

"It drove my father to distraction. He would always be checking for intruders or burglars and there was never anyone there."

Sadly, economics dictated that as a youngster Eva was frequently left alone in this ominous house.

"My parents both worked until late at night. I was terrified to be in that house by myself even when I was a teenager. The noises would scare me no end. I would often spend the time waiting for my parents to come home with my back pressed against the wall—otherwise I would continually have to look over my shoulder. I knew that there was someone else in the house with me."

Some activities were almost guaranteed to bring a response from the unseen, unpleasant and unwelcome resident poltergeist.

"Very often when I would sit down to play the piano in the living room, there would be an enormous crash."

Eva reported the crash sounded like wood splintering at the foot of the stairs. "I would jump and go to see what happened, but there was never anything to show what could have caused the noise."

Occasionally, the ghost would manifest itself as an apparition. It happened most frequently during Eva's adolescence, a coincidence that fits an expected pattern with hauntings. Ghosts are often drawn to sources of energy, and the abundance of hormonal energy present in maturing bodies is a magnet for phantoms.

"Several times over a period of years when I woke up at night, particularly when I was a teenager, I would see a middle-aged man with brown hair standing near the foot of my bed. He never said anything."

A sleep-induced hallucination? Probably not, because Eva's mother had her own similar experience with the ghost.

"My mother saw the same man in broad daylight. She had fallen asleep in the living room on an armchair during the afternoon. She was awakened by somebody squeezing her fingertips. When she looked to see who it was, she saw this man very clearly."

At the time, Eva's mother had no idea that what she was witnessing wasn't a being of this realm. The woman later reported that the image she saw looked "as if he were a real person." The apparition was silent but somehow compelled her to "follow ... him [as he] moved from the living room to the kitchen."

Within seconds of joining her unexpected and uninvited guest in the kitchen, the astonished woman realized that she was watching a ghost.

"On reaching the back door he dissolved and it was only then that she realized he wasn't real," Eva related and added that the experience had understandably "made a very deep impression" on her mother.

The ghost in the old house on Manitoba Avenue didn't always allow himself to be seen, but he did frequently find ways to make a noisy, nerve-wracking nuisance of himself.

Eva reported that throughout their stay in the haunted house, her family heard particular noises over and over again. Despite the eventual familiarity of these sounds, none of the three members of the household was ever able to identify any of them. Other sounds, however, Eva pinpointed quite easily.

"In my room I would very often hear what sounded like someone continually bouncing a ball, followed by a peculiar scraping noise."

Whatever the ghost was doing, he must have needed to stick at it because Eva reported, "This would go on for hours."

Electrical appliances in haunted houses will frequently operate strangely. Stories of ghosts with apparent preferences for certain T.V. shows are actually fairly common, as are stories about electric clocks running backwards or starting or stopping for no apparent reason. Eva's bedroom alarm clock occasionally acted oddly but what is especially interesting here is that hers was not an electric clock but one that required manual winding.

"When I sat studying in my room, a few times my wind-up alarm clock would get quieter and quieter and stop and then, without anyone having touched it in between, [would] start up again later."

In true poltergeist fashion, the family's paranormal resident liked to play tricks on its hosts.

"During the years there were many instances of things falling without explanation, particularly pictures and decorations that were hung on the walls. Things would even fall off tables. Small objects throughout the house would disappear, only to reappear again in another place."

Sadly, Eva's parents placed the blame for these hijinks on the girl, reasoning no one else was home at the time.

In 1964 an "apport"—an object seemingly materialized out of nowhere—appeared. Like most documented apports, this one was a small object but there the similarity to other apports ended. Instead of being the sort of trinket that is typical of this phenomenon, the object, which appeared in Eva's house, was a splinter of bone. To this day the woman has no way of explaining the fragment's sudden appearance. She can only make vague, rather gruesome guesses based on the fact that the splinter had been found at the top of the stairs in front of the closet door.

"I always had the impression that whatever it was that lived in the house was headquartered in the sealed space behind the closet at the head of the stairs. For some reason when the house was built, a space was closed in on the second floor that was bounded on two sides by the outside walls and on the remaining sides by my room, the closet and my parents' bedroom. We never opened this space to see what, if anything, was in there, although I often wondered."

That area of the house served as a background for a little demonstration of energy and power that Eva and her mother witnessed.

"My mother wanted to take some pictures, to use up the end of a roll of film. She asked me to stand at the base of the stairs, pointed the camera at me and set off the flashgun, which gave off an unnaturally bright flash. She tried again but [this time] nothing happened. It was then that she discovered that she had forgotten to load the battery pack into the flashgun—therefore it could not possibly have flashed when it did."

Eva and her parents lived in the house haunted by an angry spirit for more than twenty-five years before moving on. All three people were relieved to be leaving. "Both my parents and I agreed that the presence was not friendly or well-meaning. We sold the house in 1976 and I was extremely glad to get away from it."

Happily for Eva's family, the spirit did not follow them to their new home. That same fact, however, was not good news for the property's new owners.

"Less than a month later, the new owners of the old house started to complain about it. The worst thing was a sudden deep flood of black water in the basement that seemed to have no cause. This had never happened to us when we lived there and this area was high and dry. There had been no storm to account for the water."

Perhaps the ghost was angry that his long-time roommates had deserted him.

In 1992 a coincidence occurred that would likely never have been noted if the house hadn't had such an effect on Eva and her family.

"My mother was diagnosed unexpectedly with incurable cancer. A few days later I heard on the news that the old house where we had lived in the north end had burned down."

The experience of growing to adulthood in a haunted house would certainly make a profound difference on anyone's personality. Eva Pip summed it up with simple eloquence when she said, "As for me, I have become a lifetime believer in the existence of a dimension that has laws which we do not understand."

Souls Congregate Here

During the early days of the twentieth century, Winnipeg land developer Mark Fortune amassed a fortune through his far-sighted real-estate dealings. Despite the adverse reactions of many detractors, Fortune was convinced that Winnipeg's Portage Avenue could become an important business thoroughfare. He acted on his convictions and, by investing heavily in the downtown core, became a very wealthy man.

Despite his enormous wealth, home and family life remained the most important components of Fortune's life. In 1911, reflecting both his devotion to his loved ones and his wealth, he built a magnificent home for himself, his wife, Mary and their six children. The Fortune family's luxurious residence was located at 393 Wellington Crescent, a prestigious address even in those days. Sadly, neither Mark Fortune nor any of his loved ones were able to enjoy the wealth he'd accumulated for long—as a matter of fact, not for one day past April 14,1912. It was on this day that the ship *Titanic* hit an iceberg and sunk to the bottom of the North Atlantic.

Had the Fortunes not chosen to be passengers on the "unsinkable" ship's maiden voyage, the *Titanic* might only have taken 1520 souls down to their icy, black, watery graves. But as fate would have it, the final death toll was 1522, for Mark Fortune and his son Charles, as well as the family's entire fortune in negotiable assets, vanished into the depths of the North Atlantic.

As Mark and Charles Fortune stood alongside hundreds of other people congregated on the deck of the *Titanic* singing "Abide With Me," Mrs. Fortune and her daughters Ethel, Alice and Mabel were hustled into lifeboats, set adrift from certain death and, some hours later, picked up by the *Carpathia*, a ship that had been travelling nearby and had rescued all *Titanic* survivors. The surviving Fortunes, along with hundreds of others, were taken to New York. Eventually, the female members of the Fortune family made their way back to the beloved Wellington Crescent home where they lived until 1920 when they could no longer afford to maintain the large and expensive house.

"I'm not sure why the man would have taken [virtually] his entire fortune with him," my story source, whom we shall call Pam Green, admitted. "But that's apparently what happened. All the family's wealth went to the bottom of the sea that night."

In 1988, not long after Pam moved into her house near the former Fortune residence in the Wellington Crescent area, she began to sense that there was something even more special than she had first appreciated about the old place. She sensed what she suspected was a presence in her home.

A researcher both by nature and profession, Pam decided to do a bit of historical investigation. She determined that her house, like the houses of her immediate neighbours, was built around 1906, meaning that it would have been under construction at approximately the same time that Mark Fortune was building his home. She surmised that the long-deceased land developer would have been in her house during the course of a day's business.

By now, though, it was more specific information Pam was after to solve the puzzle of her unique real-estate investment. While acknowledging that her investigative efforts netted some entertaining results, she was still not much farther ahead in determining whether or not she was living in a haunted house.

Pam's archival studies revealed not only the dramatic circumstances under which Mark and Charles Fortune had met their untimely deaths, but went on to describe how that tragedy had directly caused the death of the family wealth. She was also able to find a description of Mark Fortune's physical appearance. It was recorded that the man had been dark-haired and heavily set.

While all of this information was undeniably interesting, it really didn't do much to satisfy Pam Green's curiosity about her house. She continued to sense at least one presence in her house while more and more frequently she wondered if perhaps there weren't at least two other spirits residing with her. Partly for this reason, and partly as a birthday gift to a friend, Pam invited some friends to her home as well as a man well-known for his clairvoyance.

This psychically sensitive man gave private readings for Pam and each one of her guests. He had absolutely no problem picking up on the Greens' ethereal house-mate. The psychic explained that the spirit was a "big guy" and "a man at a desk" who "loves books." Pam immediately noted dramatic similarities between the paranormal description of her resident ghost and the physical description of the area's land developer who drowned. From then on, she began to mentally collect all the bits and pieces she could of the presence in her home.

"He liked the library [in the house]," Green told me. "I've also discovered him at the end of my bed."

As with many hauntings, this particular one has not proven to be permanent.

"His energy is now gone," she stated simply.

That loss, however, did not mean that Pam was living in a spirit-free zone—far from it.

"The house has two more prominent presences," Pam continued. "I'm a night person and often when I'm baking late at night I sense a presence with me [but] when I turned to look towards it, there was nothing there. I'd just think, 'Isn't that odd?'"

But Pam's curiosity had been aroused and she began to concentrate on seeing the presence that she had, thus far, only sensed.

"I knew there was something there," she told me.

This conviction was strengthened when Pam hosted a gathering of friends, all of whom were interested in psychic phenomenon. Collectively, the group sensed a male presence in the house. This consensus helped Pam focus on actually seeing the spirit and before too long her efforts were rewarded—she was able to see the entity as speckles in a shaft of light.

Since those first months, Pam has made a point to learn as much as she possibly can about the spirits who share her home. She speaks of them both with evident fondness.

"His name is John and I think he's a large man. He loves sweets. He loves to watch me bake," Pam added before continuing. "The other presence, Alice, was a young native girl who came [many years ago] from a residential school to work in this house as a maid. I have had dreams about her. I know it was her because I've seen her photo. She was a lovely ... girl with clear eyes and round cheekbones. She's wearing a white dress, not a native outfit."

Like Mark Fortune, the energy that was Alice has, by now, left but this does not mean that John is alone in the spirit sanctuary of Pam Green's home. Pam explains that she has since sensed and then seen other energies in the house.

"I wear a lot of heavy jewellery. One day I was in the kitchen and my necklace dropped to the floor. It had a good strong clasp, it could not have just come undone," Pam explained, before adding that she was sure it was one of her resident spirit's ways of looking for attention.

Pam Green certainly doesn't mind such an occasional inconvenience caused by living in a spirit-filled house.

"I believe they know that I'm a friendly spirit and I acknowledge their presence. In their world, as in mine, souls like to congregate to visit, to remember what was. Now we do it together," she told me.

Clearly Pam Green is a person who not only accepts but enjoys the fact that she lives in a haunted house.

Knock, Knock. Who's There?

Because so much of my research is historical, I'm often amused when people comment that there seems to be increased attention to the paranormal in recent times. While absolutely agreeing that interest is currently extremely high, I frequently point out that in almost every decade of the twentieth century news of some ghostly episode has made the front page of mainstream, daily newspapers. The following story, which ran in the January 5, 1951, issue of the *Winnipeg Free Press* under the headline, "GHOST OR JOKESTER?" is an excellent example of such an occurrence.

For some days before the article ran, tenants in an apartment building on Winnipeg's Redwood Avenue had been frightened by phantom sounds that they had heard coming through their walls. The ghostly knocking followed something of a routine, generally starting in the early evening and continuing on into the wee hours of the morning. The apparent haunting was enough of a concern to those involved that, having exhausted their own investigative powers, they called the police.

A gentleman identified as A. Konyk, a resident in one of the affected apartments, explained that despite an intensive, two-hour-long search, police officers turned up no clues.

Obvious explanations, such as hot water pipes in the wall banging, were quickly ruled out by a thorough check of the building's mechanical systems. The result of that particular search didn't much surprise any of the frightened tenants for the eerie sounds had consistently shown themselves to be backed by something approaching intelligence or at least the power to reason and therefore respond appropriately.

Konyk's wife demonstrated this quirk for a visiting reporter by requesting that the presence knock four times. It did. Next she rapped on that section of the wall twice herself. The phantom mimicked the woman's actions. Hoping to take advantage of the spirit's apparently obedient nature, the woman ordered the "thing," as she had come to call it, to leave and not come back. As there was no follow-up article, perhaps the noisy knocker did just that.

An Angry Apparition

According to an article in the November 24, 1978, edition of the *Winnipeg Free Press*, a family named Winter, tenants in a haunted house on Pritchard Avenue, had recently been forced to flee from their home. They'd taken all they could of sharing their home with an angry spirit.

Mrs. Winter explained that she'd looked into the history of the house and discovered that some time ago a man had taken his own life on the second storey of the house. Upon speaking with a former tenant of the house, she was able to confirm that they'd both seen an apparition of a man on the second floor.

The sightings themselves hadn't been enough to make the first woman move from the place. She stayed on until the night she felt herself being strangled "by invisible hands." Understandably, the attack had frightened her so badly that she had made arrangements to move out at once.

Mrs. Winter, along with her three young children, had been "plagued by strange happenings" such as objects "unexplainably crashing to the floor." They had also been frightened by voices they'd heard when they knew that there was no one besides themselves in the house.

Realizing how badly traumatized the family was by their haunted house experiences, Mrs. Winter's mother had offered them temporary accommodation and the landlord had agreed to excuse the terrified family from its rental obligations. Others, however, had not been so kind. While the Winters were making arrangements to move their belongings out of the haunted house, vandals broke in and badly damaged both the house and the Winters' possessions—or so the report in the newspaper goes.

I wonder if they thought to consider that the destruction wrought on the place might have been an "inside job," perpetrated by a ragingly angry ghost.

The Ghost from the Closet

Experiencing the paranormal is evidently a profoundly moving occurrence. The numbers of people patiently waiting to talk to me after I'd spent the evening reading to people from my ghost story books used to surprise me. Often a dozen or so seemingly disparate listeners hang back long after the rest of the audience has left the hall. I quickly learned that, without exception, these people have encountered a ghost at some point in their lives and feel the need to talk to someone about their experiences.

Many of them have kept their supernatural encounter completely to themselves for years. Whether the experience they finally wished to unburden themselves of happened recently or decades ago, strong emotions are still evident in their retelling. Many people have surprised themselves by weeping as they spoke of their encounters with spirits. Evidently, they desperately need to share their secret with someone and I seem to be the ideal recipient. Not only am I a stranger to them but even better, I'm obviously a stranger who's heard similar stories.

The following story is a classic example of this phenomenon. Its route to my desk was an intriguing one. My friend and colleague, Jo-Anne Christensen was researching her book, *Ghost Stories of British Columbia*. She sprinkled requests for stories around B.C. radio stations, newspapers, libraries and museums. An eighty-year-old woman, now living in Burnaby, B.C., replied with a first-hand account of having lived in a haunted house in the late 1920s.

Even though she experienced the ghost nearly seventy years ago, Margaret Jerome was still able to supply an amazing number of details, including the exact address on Roseberry Street in St. James. No one else in Margaret's family ever saw the ghost but as she was the only member of the household in her early teens that isn't too surprising. Ghostly sightings are often reported in conjunction with the hormonal turmoil of puberty.

Many decades later, Margaret wrote that as she lay sleeping in the room she shared with her younger sister she would often waken to the sight of a man coming out of the bedroom closet. The poor youngster huddled, paralyzed with fear, as she watched the image, holding a knife in his raised hand, move across the floor to the doorway.

"I would scream," she recalled. "And my younger sister would wake up and look everywhere for the man."

"There's no one here," Margaret's sibling assured her badly frightened sister.

Despite the reassurances Margaret reported, "I'd be so badly shaken I had to go to my parents' room for the rest of the night."

"[This] happened many nights," the writer recalled. She might have spent a severely sleep-deprived adolescence if the family hadn't moved. The new house was just across the street but, much to Margaret's relief, the ghost didn't follow her. He stayed within his realm.

After researching the history of their former home, the family understood not only why it was haunted but also why the ghost didn't follow them. That background check also explained why, on the day they moved into the house, they had found a bloodstain on the dining room floor.

There had been a murder in that house on Roseberry Street.

By now the only question left to ponder is whether the threatening-looking ghost that Margaret saw so often was the murderer or the victim.

Two Atlantic Avenue Stories

While searching for Manitoba ghost stories, I stumbled across some rather odd and intriguing coincidences. Of course, many of those chance similarities did not hold up under closer scrutiny, but I found the ones that did, provocative indeed. I was amazed, for instance, to find three stories connected with the word "Atlantic." The first involved the sinking of the *Titanic* on the North Atlantic (p. 55). The last two had nothing to do with the ocean but rather Atlantic Avenue in Winnipeg.

The first Atlantic Avenue ghost story I found was reported in a book called *Canada's PSI Century*, which was released in honour of Canada's centennial year. The woman who reported the following paranormal experiences identified herself only by the initials "D.R." and indicated that, at that time, she resided in East Kildonan.

Some time in the early 1960s, tragedy struck D.R.'s family when her eldest son, a teenager, died. Although she did not report the cause of the lad's death, D.R. did, however, add that a mere six months later her father had also passed away unexpectedly. Naturally enough, the woman was devastated. To help herself cope with her grief, she began pondering philosophical issues that, up until then, she'd considered herself too busy to dwell on. Was there life after death? she wondered. Searching for the answer, D.R. read as many books as she could find on the subject. Although she found that her readings did provide her with some much-needed emotional comfort, the information did nothing to satisfy her intellectual curiosity; this absence was decidedly frustrating to the grieving woman.

Despite the tragedies and the toll they'd taken on her, D.R. tried to get on with her life as best she was able. Often, when she found time heavy on her hands, the woman would while away parts of her day at the piano. She was doing just that on the evening of September 30, 1964. That particular night, she was completely wrapped up in her music. It took the sound of a roaring fire in the fireplace directly behind her to startle her away from the keyboard.

She swung around from the piano to face the fireplace wondering what she would see. Would she be greeted by the glow of the fire she had so clearly heard? If so, who on earth could have lit it? But the fireplace was empty, except for the cold, charred remains of the family's last fire some days before. Despite this visual proof that there was no fire, D.R. continued to hear the popping and snapping of a fiercely burning fire.

Because she had recently been investigating the world of the supernatural, it crossed D.R.'s mind that she was experiencing an entity's attempt to contact her. For several more minutes she stared at the cold, lifeless fireplace while listening to the sounds of a robust, crackling fire. No matter how hard she tried, D.R. was unable to shake the strange and seemingly contradictory experience from her mind. Even the following day, she could think of little else as she went about her day's activities. Suddenly, she was overcome by an urge to sit down with a paper and a pencil. For a few seconds she just sat there, pen poised on the paper, but frankly, feeling a little silly. Then, she felt the pen move. Oddly, the pen seemed to be taking her hand with it, instead of the other way around. At first the movement was so slight and felt so strange that she decided she'd only imagined it. Within mere moments, however, the movement had become definite and purposeful.

The first recognizable word that came through with D.R.'s "automatic writing" was a name. Much to her surprise, however, the name belonged to neither her recently deceased son nor her father, but rather it was the nickname of a woman friend who had also died in the past few months. Slowly, the spirit wrote out her message using D.R. as both the medium as well as the recipient. D.R. didn't realize that this experience was only the beginning of her adventures into the paranormal.

As time went on, the automatic-writing messages came more frequently. Both D.R. and her deceased friend became increasingly adept at communicating between the two planes of existence. Eventually, the friend even brought D.R.'s son to greet her.

The grieving mother found great comfort in her newly discovered abilities and tried to share them with her very skeptical husband. The man would have none of it, however, and D.R. was forced to explore this new dimension in her life by herself. Accordingly, the woman began to make changes in her life, including the decision to attend a spiritualist church. During the Mother's Day service, the minister broke with his usual tradition to announce that he saw a young lad beside D.R. and that the boy had informed him that she was his mother. Perhaps sensing that his mother would be dubious of the minister's claim, the son's spirit began to supply the man with information that would prove his claim. The presence attested that his father had once worked for the Hydro. As D.R.'s husband had only worked there for a very short time more than twenty years before, it would have been impossible for the minister to know that himself. The woman was now convinced that, with the help of her new church affiliation, her son had come to visit her on Mother's Day.

The following Sunday she also attended a service and was rewarded with another remarkable visit from her deceased son. To prove his identity this time, the spirit gave the minister a single word—"Atlantic." Initially, D.R. was extremely puzzled by the reference for, at first, she associated the word only with the ocean. It wasn't until the spirit gave the minister a numerical prefix to the word Atlantic that D.R. finally made the correct connection—her son was giving the address of the house where the family had lived for the first two years of his life.

Perhaps realizing that these word clues were an effective way to prove his identity, the woman's son next communicated the word "Aikins." After a moment the presence followed that word with a three-digit number and then repeated "Aikins." He had given her the address of the home the family had moved to after leaving the house on Atlantic Avenue.

Thanks to the persistence of her son's ghost, D.R. was able to find some badly needed comfort.

The following story also involves Atlantic Avenue—namely, a haunted house situated on Atlantic Avenue. A young couple named George and Susan Scull reportedly purchased the place from an elderly widow named Mrs. Soar. The woman sold the home with understandable reluctance. Her husband had built the house himself and they'd lived there happily together until the day he died. By now, however, the widow had to admit that keeping the place up by herself was not only too much work but also something of an exercise in futility. More comfortable alternatives were available to her if she sold the place and recouped their long-standing real-estate investment.

It was Susan Scull who first saw the ghost in their newly purchased home. Responding to a cry in the night from one of her children, she got up to see what the problem might be. There, standing at the end of one of her children's beds, was an apparition—the nearly transparent manifestation of an old man.

Mrs. Scull reported that she couldn't feel frightened by the ghostly sighting because the man's spirit seemed so full of love and tenderness. When the woman reported her experience to her husband, his reaction was quite different from hers. George Scull found his wife's anecdote hilarious. He thought he'd never heard anything quite so funny in his entire life. And that was the high-spirited attitude Mr. Scull maintained for several days. It wasn't until the morning that George Scull walked into his own kitchen and saw the late Mr. Soar calmly sitting there that his wife's experience became something more than a joke to the man.

Soar's ghost must have exuded the same warmth to George as he did to Susan for neither reported feeling afraid of the presence. The phantom continued to visit the Scull's home periodically until the early 1980s. Shortly after the couple noticed that the supernatural guest had stopped appearing, they heard that old Mrs. Soar had finally died. Evidently, the loving apparition no longer had any reason to call upon his former home on Winnipeg's Atlantic Avenue.

Historic Hamilton House

A place where spirits once visited will not, apparently, always be haunted. Of course, we believers, who also happen to be slightly timid folk, must not take too much comfort from that fact because the reverse implication could also be true: just because you are happily living in an "unhaunted" home today is no guarantee that it will always be a ghost-free zone.

The former home of Dr. T. G. Hamilton, at Henderson Highway and McIntosh Avenue in Winnipeg, is an excellent example of a house with a past that included ghostly guests but a present that is decidedly quiet. The stately old home has long since been subdivided so that it now contains apartments and a shop called the "Olive Branch." According to the people associated with the store, the building is only "haunted" by the legends and rumours that continue to swirl around the place. The Olive Branch's association with the Mennonite Church might, of course, have something to do with this firmly held conviction.

No one with any knowledge of the building's history could reasonably deny that at one time, at least—from the end of WWI until the mid-1930s—a veritable smorgasbord of paranormal activity took place in the Hamilton home.

In addition to his position as a highly esteemed Elmwood-area physician, Dr. Hamilton, who also served as president of the Manitoba Medical Association for a time, was considered a pivotal member of the local Presbyterian church and was an influential provincial politician. Hamilton's progressive beliefs led him to back some highly contentious and liberal bills—in one case going as far as supporting the radical premise that women should be allowed to vote.

Understandably, Hamilton was considered to have been politically precocious, but he carried his unconventional philosophies even further—into the paranormal. Author John Robert Colombo, in his book *Mysterious Canada*, states that Hamilton could well be considered "the most important psychical researcher Canada has ever known."

Hamilton was fascinated by the world of the spirits and was determined to discover whether or not communication between the realm of the living and that of the deceased was possible. Towards this end, he held many seances and other spiritual gatherings in his home. His remarkable successes drew national and eventually worldwide attention.

To some degree this recognition was the result of timing. Interest in things paranormal had suddenly swept the world. Everyone, it seemed, wanted to communicate with the dead. Many, including those attending the Hamilton seances, did so through "table-tipping," a paranormal activity that, at the time, was considered to be little more than a parlour game. Through table-tipping, communication with the "other side" was accomplished by seating a group of people in a circle and having them place their hands on a small table that had been situated in their midst. (Placing their hands on top of the table served the dual purpose of accounting for everyone's hands—thereby ruling out "sleight of hand"—and also on concentrating the participants' energy.)

Once they were so arranged, the group would focus on contacting spirits, and they often succeeded. Presumably responding to the same mysterious force that drives the planchette of an Ouija board, the host's otherwise standard table would "tip." In response to a system pre-determined by the people attending, spirits would lift the table a few centimetres off the floor, angle slightly and, with one or two legs, tap or knock on the floor. In its simplest terms, one knock would usually represent a positive answer, two a negative reply.

Predictably, after some success with this method, participants wanted more detailed communication with the entities. To answer this demand, a system was developed where one tap stood for the letter "A," two for the letter "B" and so on. Anyone involved in such a ritual must have hoped the spirit they contacted had not been a linguist in life. Sitting through too many words like "zymurgy" or even "wizard" could strain the most patient person's resources. Perhaps this complication is part of the reason table-tipping became accepted as a form of entertainment. Rather than spending a social evening dancing, telling stories or playing cards with friends, people invited each other into their homes for the expressed purpose of attempting to contact spirits.

These types of spiritual get-togethers were so widely accepted that even Canada's prime minister at the time, William Lyon Mackenzie King (1874–1950), frequently contacted the ghosts of his loved ones. It is probably a blessing that Canadians had been unaware their country was being led by a man who not only communicated regularly with his dead dog but was also privy to direction from Biblical characters. (King was prime minister for three terms: 1921–26; 1926–30; and 1935–48.)

Dr. Hamilton once hosted a visit from Prime Minister King who was most impressed with the researcher's work and methods. Because Dr. Hamilton's background was in medicine, he strove to make his pursuit of the paranormal as scientific as he could. Towards this end, whenever possible, Hamilton used the technology of the day, specifically, photography. His photographic efforts were dramatically rewarded with some very provocative photos. These pictures included images of spirits who had apparently been called forth by the living participants involved in the Hamilton House seances.

News of Dr. Hamilton's successes at summoning spirits soon spread and actually led to him discontinuing the sessions out of concern for his medical practice. Despite the acceptance of spiritualism during that era, he worried that his journeys into the world of the occult would diminish his role as a respected healer. His concerns and the suspension of his experiments turned out to be short lived.

In January 1923, friends convinced the man to give table-tipping another try. At that session he received a clear message of

Former Prime Minister William Lyon Mackenzie King shared an interest in the paranormal with Dr. Hamilton, and he once visited Hamilton House.

encouragement from whatever force was communicating. The table levitated, tilted and knocked against the floor in a systematic, organized and apparently understood way. The spirits had spoken. It was clear to Hamilton and his friends that the spirits wanted Hamilton to continue his investigations. He did continue, finding that his popularity as a physician actually grew from his spiritual investigations. In addition, people considered him an expert in the field of the paranormal and Hamilton became very much in demand as a lecturer.

There is great justification for this recognition if only based on the man's successes, but it was his methods that were even more impressive. His scrupulous research is detailed in a book he wrote, entitled *Intention and Survival.* The documentation of a seance held in the early part of 1930 demonstrates the strictly controlled circumstances under which these sessions were conducted. There is an affidavit signed by an uninvolved observer, a respected lawyer named Isaac Pitblado. The man described in detail not only the session and his reason for involvement, but also the complicated procedures used to eliminate the possibility of the session's being a hoax.

Pitblado's involvement had been requested by a spirit named "Walter." This ghost had been contacted in a previous session and had specified who he wanted as an objective observer to his reappearance. The report Pitblado penned about the seance went on for more than a thousand words, most of which attested to the sophisticated measures taken to ensure the legitimacy of the spiritual contact.

Pitblado described how the room where the seance was to be held had been thoroughly searched for possible aids to a hoax. The room had then been double-locked and actually sealed by means of knotted, unbroken pieces of string with stickers adhered to them. These stickers were signed by two respected members of the community, proving that the room had been secured. As Pitblado pointed out in his writing, even if there had been no locks on the door, the fact that the seals remained intact proved that the room hadn't been entered since it had last been examined. Despite this assurance, Pitblado thoroughly searched the room himself, including all of the photographic equipment set up to, hopefully, record the appearance of an apparition.

Once all of that was accomplished, Pitblado searched each man before allowing anyone to enter the recently opened room. None of the participants were allowed to enter with their jackets on or even their shirt sleeves rolled down. Everything that the men carried into the room with them was itemized, although these objects amounted to little more than cigarette lighters and coins.

Having assured himself that neither the room nor any of participants were equipped to perpetrate a sham, Pitblado let the seance begin.

Walter, the spirit who had requested that Mr. Pitblado attend the session, made his presence known almost immediately. As Walter's stated purpose was only to substantiate his own ghostly existence, he provided such proof without delay. Once all of the men around the table were holding hands, Walter asked that Pitblado join hands with the medium in attendance. The medium was already holding Dr. Hamilton's right hand and a Mr. Cross's left hand. Pitblado's hands were then placed on top of the other two.

The man designated as the photographer in the group took a series of photos immediately after those instructions were followed. After the seance, Pitblado accompanied Hamilton, with the photographic plates, to a darkroom where they stayed until the developing process had been completed. The pictures turned out even better than had been hoped. All the people at the seance photographed well—even Walter. Yes, much to everyone's satisfaction, there was clearly the image of an extra person in each of the photographs. By combining his own spiritual power with the day's technology, Walter, the ghost, had managed to prove his very existence. The controlled conditions under which this experiment was conducted certainly make its integrity convincing.

The success also encouraged the group to continue its work and to regularly incorporate cameras into the sessions. The hundreds of photos taken during these seances are now part of The University of Manitoba's archival collections. Some photographs show tables flying through the air and others illustrate the phenomenon of "ectoplasm" or "teleplasm." Both words define a white fluid that traditionally manifests itself around a medium's head. This material occasionally contained likenesses of whatever spirit had been summoned by those involved in the seance.

In short, Dr. Hamilton's successes in the field of paranormal investigation were astounding. As recently as forty years ago, the *Free Press* ran a thirteen-part series, written by Dr. Hamilton's daughter, about his pioneering work. In its introduction, the newspaper implied that the series would be something of a public service, providing background information about the field of the paranormal. As the writer of the January 18, 1958, introduction put it, "The average reader, without special training or experience in the subject, is likely to find himself lacking any satisfactory criterion to distinguish the work of value from what may indeed be nothing more than self-deception or even fraud."

Today's reader can extrapolate from those mildly condescending sentiments and from the fact that the newspaper was running such a long series of articles, that interest in spiritualism was, by the late 1950s, high once again. (Interest had died down during the Great Depression.)

The articles described how a woman named Mary M. had frequently acted as the medium for seances held at Hamilton's house. Once in trance, Mary M. became "Dawn," a personality possessing abilities well beyond Mary's scope. The spirit named Walter often spoke through Dawn during these sessions but others from "beyond" also spoke through the psychic. Frederic Myers, a scholar and paranormal pioneer who worked in Britain until his death in 1901, visited as did author Robert Louis Stevenson (1850–94). The latter identified himself as only one of the writers in the spirit world who was intent on teaching those on the physical plane that there is not only survival after death, but the potential for communication between the two planes.

Another of the presences to identify itself was that of W.T. Stead. This man had been a renowned psychic investigator who had published a book of "automatic writing." (A phenomenon that occurs when the writer, often a medium, is in a trance. The information that is automatically written in this altered state is

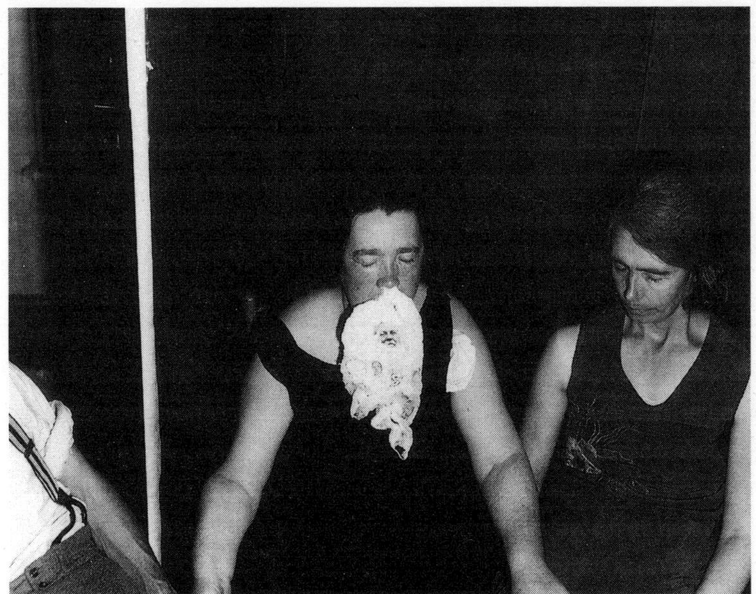

"Ectoplasm," or "teleplasm," is a white fluid that usually manifests itself around a medium's head.

often beyond the knowledge of the person writing, and is usually considered to be from a spirit or other supernatural being.) Sadly, Stead's research and life were cut short by his death on April 14, 1912, when the luxury liner *Titanic* sank. He, too, wanted to assure all of those involved that the loss of the physical body did not mark the end of a spirit's life.

Some spirits kept their anonymity but gave Dawn and the others specific instructions on how to further communicate. One of those spirits requested that Dawn be given a pen and paper for the next session so that he might dictate a message through her. When she was properly equipped, the woman began a session of automatic writing in which the spirit, working through her, described the world beyond as being quite similar to the world of the living. The presence informed those people attending that "The spirit world ... is the abode of undeveloped spirits, those who have not long left the body and those who by the law of the spirit life have not risen to higher spheres. …"

The entity went on to describe how he had arrived at his current plane of existence: "I was taken into a mist like a great cloud [which] encircled me." Much to the disappointment of anyone looking forward to "purer" times in the "great beyond," the spirit reported, "There is as much superstition and bigotry on the subject of spirit communion among spirits as among those in the flesh."

The entities also communicated with the group by drawing likenesses of the spirits. Once transformed from Mary to Dawn by way of a trance, the medium had an admirable artistic bent and frequently drew a portrait of the person communicating with her.

By the mid-1930s much of the interest in the phenomenon had faded. The world was suffering a most severe economic downturn—the Great Depression had begun. People deeply concerned with how to feed their families had little interest in the paranormal. Coincidentally, Dr. Hamilton died in the spring of 1935. He did not live to see a resurgence of interest in the subject he had found so intriguing and in which he had conducted so many carefully documented and controlled experiments.

Those who had been closest to Dr. Hamilton and his work continued to hold seances after the man's death. Not surprisingly, the ghost of the doctor even attended a few of those sessions himself. The August 12, 1938, edition of the *Free Press* ran a small article about a former political colleague of Hamilton's who was attempting to communicate with spirits when he heard a familiar voice:

"Is that you?" the man inquired.

Hamilton assured his former associate that it was and that he was well and accompanied by author Sir Arthur Conan Doyle. This news was not startling to anyone who had known Hamilton, for the author of the Sherlock Holmes stories had an enthusiastic interest in the supernatural and the two men had known and respected each other in life.

Dr. Hamilton, Winnipeg's physician, politician and paranormal investigator, was clearly a man ahead of his time. It is easy to imagine how he would not only enjoy, but contribute to today's growing collection of knowledge about the supernatural world.

Considering what a rich venue for ghostly activity Hamilton House once was, I was disappointed to learn that today it is quiet, apparently devoid of spirits. Perhaps that emptiness, however, is only because most of the time there is no one in the house to beckon the spirits.

A conversation with local psychic Shelley O'Day confirmed this possibility for me. O'Day had visited Hamilton House at the invitation of Dr. Hamilton's daughter, Margaret Hamilton Bach. Miss O'Day recalled perceiving the image of a cello between herself and her hostess. When she mentioned this to the former Miss Hamilton, the woman was not at all surprised. Although there hadn't been a cello in the house for years, her deceased brother had played the instrument. Perhaps he's just waiting for some of the other spirits that once populated his family home to return and visit into eternity.

Chapter 2

GHOSTS IN PUBLIC

"Murray the Ghost"

Collecting ghost stories can occasionally be frustrating. Often it seems that just when you think you've stumbled upon an answer you've been searching for, you also turn up another question. Why is one particular place haunted and yet another seemingly not? Why does one person's spirit live on while another's soul might never be heard from again? In the following story, it's tempting to think that there's a fairly obvious answer to both those questions.

What is now the administration building for The University of Manitoba's Delta Marsh Field Station was originally a hunting lodge. As far back as the Dirty Thirties, wealthy hunters from all over the world travelled to the south shore of Lake Manitoba to stay at Mallard Lodge. Clark Gable and Cary Grant were two celebrities who availed themselves of both the duck hunting and the hospitality associated with the privately run lodge.

Mallard Lodge's caretaker, Murray, was one of those on hand to cater to the wealthy gentlemen's every need. Apparently, Murray loved his job and, for more than thirty years, did it well. Of course, that was a long time ago and Murray's been dead for years by now. Despite the indisputable fact of his passing, there continues to be strong indications that the former caretaker remains in residence, working away into eternity.

Haunted Mallard Lodge

Russ Mead, who has worked as the Delta Marsh station manager since the mid-1980s, has always been aware of a ghostly presence in the lodge.

"Ah, yes, Murray, the ghost," Russ Mead said with a chuckle when I called in the spring of 1997 to ask him about the resident entity. "He hasn't been active too much lately and that's a little surprising because I was here alone a lot with the flooding and all. Of course, maybe I was just too zonked and tired to be able to detect him [under those circumstances], but apparently we do have a bonafide ghost here. He's a friendly ghost, Murray, the caretaker. He used to be a lot more active than he is now. If you were able to trace the ghost history of this place, you'd find he was around most when there wasn't a lot of people here. When this place was first a field station, there were lots of reports of Murray's activities. He would open and close doors. Turn on faucets and lights. Just before that, the place had been nearly abandoned for a while."

To prove his point about Murray preferring to show off when only a few people are around to witness his hijinks, Russ related that over a previous August long weekend a man and his girlfriend had to stay at the station alone.

"The ghost was there. He did lots. The girl saw his figure at a window and he also rang the bell," Russ recalled, before explaining that causing the station bell to ring is no simple feat. "It's on a wire pole and it takes quite a bit to ring it."

As a biological field station, the Delta Marsh is often a temporary home to scientists. Those trained to observe and record impartially are generally not folks given to flights of fancy. Despite this a graduate science student named Michael Goodyear had an experience he'll likely never forget.

Mead began relating the student's experience by explaining what he knew of Goodyear. "He was a meticulous kind of guy. Not a goofball at all. He'd never be one to play a practical joke."

Russ Mead, Delta Marsh station manager

Having thus set the tone of a credible report, the station manager went on to relate that Michael Goodyear had the "closest encounter of anyone. He was in his bunk unable to sleep. He had a flashlight with him and the first thing he noticed was that it had been moved. Then he saw a skull at the end of his bed. The figure was draped. It rose up and floated over him."

Given that Goodyear was at the station to gain experience, his stay certainly served its purpose. It would be interesting to know whether the morning's visit from the apparition spurred any sudden interest in additional fields of research.

After chatting about Murray and the haunted lodge for a few minutes, the personable Russ Mead paused for a moment before adding, "I kind of wondered if Murray had been around recently because the thermostat was acting strangely but all I did was re-program it. Maybe he could have caused that, I don't know."

Given the attraction of ghosts to things electric and electronic, it's quite possible that Murray did cause the glitch although, of course, we'll never really know. What we probably can surmise accurately is that Murray is the reason the former Mallard Lodge is haunted. It would appear that this story is a case of the deceased not being aware he's dead, and it seems a safe bet that The University of Manitoba research station at Delta Marsh will remain haunted as long as Murray continues to think he's still alive.

Is There or Isn't There?

"The Walker Theatre is NOT haunted."

That sort of a reply to a question doesn't allow a lot of room for negotiation. It did, however, provoke my curiosity about the old place even further because I'd been given to understand that the haunting of the Walker Theatre was a widely accepted phenomenon. Being completely unprepared for the denial I received, I must admit to having been immediately and effectively silenced. Worse, I was sure that my total lack of response to the theatre representative's assertion would effectively destroy any hope of obtaining more information.

Much to my delight, however, the reverse proved to be true. The woman who had answered my phone call seemed to take my silence as a challenge to the veracity of her claim and she launched into a defence of her statement.

"This place isn't haunted. That's just a joke. We kid about there being a ghost here. Whenever a door slams and there's been no one around it or when things go missing for no reason we just say, 'Oh, it must be the ghost.'"

While listening to her and trying to compose myself to continue the conversation, I must admit a line from *Hamlet* did come to mind. Much like the Prince of Denmark I couldn't help but think, "The lady doth protest too much." First of all, if the place wasn't haunted, why would doors unexpectedly slam and things mysteriously go missing? And secondly, why would someone be so defensive if there had never been any indication that there was a ghost in the theatre?

The telephone conversation lasted mere seconds from that point, but after we'd said good-bye I realized that, in a backwards sort of a way, it had accomplished my purpose. I certainly had one take—and an interesting one at that—on the ghost at the Walker Theatre. Now all I had to do was ferret out proponents of the other side of the issue.

Fortunately, that didn't prove to be too difficult. My next call was to the library at the *Winnipeg Sun*. The librarian recalled that the paper had run articles about the ghost at the Walker Theatre and, better yet, the reporter who covered the stories was still an employee so the man kindly re-directed my call to her.

"I had quite an experience there," acknowledged longtime *Sun* reporter, Naomi Lakritz.

To me, this comment did not sound like the reaction one would have expected from a seasoned newspaper journalist to an ordinary assignment. After listening to the woman describe her investigation, I realized the assignment had most assuredly not been ordinary, but rather extraordinary, in every sense of the word. The "strangest assignment I've had in nearly a decade working for the *Winnipeg Sun*" was how she described it.

"The stagehands [at the Walker] had talked about ghosts. My editor originally had it planned that I would stay overnight in the theatre," she recalled.

Fortunately for Naomi's nerves that version of the plan didn't work out. "I didn't like that idea, but then the people at the theatre said that wouldn't work anyway because of their motion detectors. If their security system wasn't turned on [including the motion detectors], then their insurance [company] wouldn't cover them if anything happened."

Naomi and her editor moved right along to "Plan B."

"I had a psychic [Shelley O'Day] go in with me and we took a tape recorder. First, we went right up to what they call the 'gods'—as high up as you can go in the theatre. We set up [a tape recorder] there and just waited for about half an hour. We didn't hear anything. Then we moved to what they call the 'fly gallery' where all the ropes [for props and curtains] hang. Shelley said she could feel cold currents, but I told her it was just a fan. We were there about thirty minutes. There was no one else in the auditorium part of the theatre except us. [There were a couple of people in the box office area.] No one came near us the whole time. When we played that tape back I couldn't believe what was [recorded] on there. There was loud banging sounds and hammering. Then there were footsteps walking across the floor to the tape recorder and away from it. Then there were more footsteps and it sounded like someone whispered 'Please' into the tape recorder."

. Naomi's description of the contradiction between the silence she and Shelley had thought they'd been surrounded by and the noises that the tape machine beside them had picked up was definitely indicative of at least one presence. She added what was stranger still "about the tape was that sometimes when you played it the sounds were on it and other times when you played it the tape was blank."

Wanting to verify that what she'd experienced wasn't a prank, Naomi questioned well-known ghost-buff Roy Bauer. He knows Shelley O'Day, knows of her remarkable talents as a psychic, as well as her definite limitations as a technician.

"I asked Roy if Shelley could somehow have set this whole thing with the tape recorder up. He told me, 'Not a chance.' He said, 'Shelley can't even program her own VCR.'"

Clearly his message was that it would have been completely unimaginable for Shelley O'Day to have purposely created the bizarre tape. I wondered what the experience had been like from

Shelley's perspective. As a psychic who is frequently called upon to determine whether or not a building is haunted, she was, of course, more matter-of-fact about the experience.

"On the tape you could hear someone pacing and out of breath. The floor [on which they were pacing] seemed like steel. We did get the spirits on tape. The spirit draws on my energy to project on tape. I picked some different people up when I was first in the theatre."

All of this certainly served to confirm the stagehands' rather vague reports of feeling stared at when they knew they were alone or feeling a presence when there was no one visible near them. Personnel also reported hearing footsteps when there was no physical way that such a sound could be made.

It's a fair guess that the ghost was a theatre buff because employee Wayne Jackson reported that, "At the end of a performance, I almost hear people clapping up there [an unoccupied tier of seats]. But it's always during an opera or something like that. I don't think ghosts appreciate rock and roll."

Tom Cochrane's music is considerably more contemporary than the ghosts likely are, which is perhaps why the spirits gave security guard Jim St. Louis such a hard time. St. Louis was to provide security for the Canadian musician's equipment while it was being stored overnight after Cochrane's concert at the Grey Cup game in Winnipeg.

St. Louis was quoted in an interview with the *Winnipeg Sun* as saying, "I made a sweep of the theatre at 3:00 a.m. with my two dogs and it was empty. But it was like someone was in there! I thought someone's now in the theatre but no one was there, for sure."

In addition he "felt someone looking at me in the basement all the time. Oh, if you'd been there you would have run out. ..."

St. Louis had received specific orders to close the two steel doors on each side of the fly gallery that sits high above the stage.

"I couldn't close the door. It was too heavy. It must weigh a couple of hundred pounds so I just left it. Then I got downstairs again and heard a big slam. I ran back up there and the door was closed."

At least now the doors that were supposed to be closed were. However, St. Louis certainly wasn't feeling any more comfortable.

As he patrolled the dressing room area, he noted that certain doors he'd been told had to stay open were closed. "The bathroom doors up there have to be kept open because it's not heated and they don't want the pipes to freeze. The door is propped open with a wedge of wood. Then you make a round and everytime, the door is closed. The wood's been kicked aside but no one's been up there. There's a total of six doors where this happens."

The man was accompanied by his dogs whom he described as, "usually outgoing dogs, and they'll wander through whatever place I'm working. But they hung around me all night. They went crazy barking."

When the doors started slamming the "boxer dog was going nuts, barking." The dogs also refused to accompany their owner when he went to the fourth floor of the theatre, which was uncharacteristic of them.

Why would the spectacular Walker Theatre be haunted? After all, it wasn't like the Manitoba Theatre Centre (see p. 97) where there was a clearcut explanation for the ghost. Winnipegger Chris Rutkowski explained in his book *Unnatural History* that "[t]heatre ghosts are quite common." Wayne Jackson, a former Walker Theatre house manager, was quoted in the *Sun* as saying, "There's a lot of talk in theatres about phantoms. I've been in theatres for many years and strange things happen." Only flyman Kenny Jackson was willing to take a stab at whom one or two of the presences might be. He connected a plaque in the theatre lobby to the hauntings. It is a memorial to the husband-and-wife acting team of Laurence Irving and Mabel Hackney. They performed at the Walker on May 23, 1914 and less than a week later "perished with 1020 others when the *S.S. Empress of Ireland* sank in the Gulf of St. Lawrence.

"[Y]ou kind of wonder," Kenny told a reporter. He is also one of the Walker employees who will admit to having witnessed "some eerie things at the Walker."

There might be some debate about whether the theatre is haunted and if it is, then by whom, but there is no doubt of the grand old lady's splendour. Constructed in 1907, the Walker was later called, "one of the finest on the American continent." During its heyday, the theatre hosted most of vaudeville's big names: Charlie Chaplin, Bob Hope, Groucho Marx, Sophie Tucker, Jimmy Durante and Georgie Jessel all strutted their stuff across the theatre's impressive stage. Until the early 1930s, it was a proud and grand entertainment hall. With the Depression, however, no one had any money for luxuries such as shows and the place fell on hard times. It was eventually seized for back taxes before re-opening as a cinema. This incarnation lasted until 1991 when the hall, restored to its original glory, became a home for live entertainment once again.

It's hoped that the spirits of the place are pleased with what their long-time home has become—even if some who work there don't recognize their ghostly existence. Of course, if the person who answered my call truly believes that there are no spirits at the Walker, I wonder why the staff makes a habit of leaving "the ghost lamp" on?

Strange Musical Strains

Ghost stories are, almost by definition, puzzling, but this one is intriguing, even set against other tales with mystical components. It is one of the best-known Winnipeg stories, and, by most fortunate coincidence, it is also one of the most thoroughly documented.

This story is about the organ in St. John's Anglican Cathedral. On a seasonally cold Sunday in December 1953, the Reverend H.J. Skynner, curate of the Cathedral, was beginning a service. It was an early service—8:00 a.m.—and so was not particularly well attended. Reverend J.O. Anderson, the Dean of Rupertsland, was one of only a dozen or so who attended that unforgettable morning service.

The service was less formal than more conventionally scheduled opportunities to worship. No musical accompaniment had been arranged. Neither the choir nor the organist, D.H. Hadfield, were in attendance. Despite this, just as the Reverend Skynner began reading a Biblical passage, a note sounded from the grand pipe organ behind him.

The sound startled the sparse congregation as much as it did the minister. All of those present could clearly see that no one was anywhere near the instrument. Besides, the note they'd heard didn't even sound as though it had come from an organ—it sounded more like a single note being played on a flute.

Only slightly dismayed by the musical interruption, Reverend Skynner proceeded with the service. To everyone's amazement, the unusual music also continued—throughout the entire service. All in attendance, including magazine publisher Ted Byfield, listened to the pleasant, but completely unfamiliar sounds.

The most obvious explanation for the odd occurrence would be wind from outside of the church blowing into the pipes. Unfortunately, that apparently logical explanation is very easy to debunk because not only was it not particularly windy that day, but only one pipe at a time sounded. If winter winds had actually been the unseen organist, the church would have been filled with a cacophony. Besides, the next day workers were called in to thoroughly inspect the instrument. All the stops, which would have prevented the wind from entering the pipes, were found to be secure. Also, it was noted at that time that less than two years prior, organ specialists Albert and Robert Blanchard had installed special stops in the twelve-hundred-pipe organ to ensure that the wind could never interfere with the sound system.

What the congregation heard during that church service was not the result of either a defective instrument or weather abnormalities. In fact, any readers who like a story with an obvious explanation had better not dwell on this one, for everyone in the church, including the minister, had a clear view of the massive organ. Certainly no human being could be playing it without being seen by the people in attendance.

To date, the reason for the strange-sounding music heard in St. John's Anglican Cathedral one chilly Sunday morning more than forty years ago continues to elude us. And that, I thought, was the whole story until I was invited to take part in a phone-in radio show on CJOB in Winnipeg. The very first caller had additional information for me about the musically spirited church. The man explained that his parents had been members of that church for a very long time and had, in the early 1960s, actually witnessed the church bells being rung by an unseen presence.

"It was definitely not the wind," the man assured me. "At the time those bells could only have been operated manually. Since then, sometime around the mid-1960s, they were automated and to my knowledge, it's never happened again."

The caller went on to explain that although the church is old, the land on which it was built was known to have been used as a graveyard in the mid-1800s. Perhaps the musical interludes were merely some long-deceased Manitoba pioneer's way of contributing to a church service in his or her own ghostly way.

Researcher W. Ritchie Benedict recently discovered what is effectively a most appropriate postscript to this story. While poring through archival newspapers, he came across a reference from the late 1800s in Wisconsin. It seems that a church organ there just as suddenly began to play strange music. Like the Winnipeg story, this organ began and ended its phantom concert without warning, precedence or follow-up.

A thought-provoking coincidence.

An Additional, Unanticipated Adventure

Jane Allan is a vivacious young woman who has grown very used to having ghosts in her life. As a child she moved, with her family, from California to Calgary and yes, you guessed it, into a house with a resident ghost. Jane was kind enough to send me an account of life in a haunted house as well as the details of a specific incident that she had experienced in her teens. I offer this background as evidence that by the time Jane visited Winnipeg she was experienced enough with ghosts that she was not easily "spooked."

It seems that in 1996 Jane's boyfriend moved from Alberta to Manitoba. Early in November of that year, she decided to surprise the young man with a visit. She splurged on a plane ticket and was very much looking forward to giving the young man a happy surprise. The day before she was to leave, Jane decided that it would be best to let her boyfriend in on the secret. As it turned out that decision was a wise one, for the man, not knowing what his girlfriend had planned, had gone ahead and made arrangements of his own for the time period she was planning to visit Winnipeg.

Only temporarily set back, Jane resorted to "Plan B." As she put it, "I had bought this plane ticket and it was not going to waste. ..." She phoned a close friend and asked her if she had any important plans to carry out over the next few days. When the reply was negative, Jane proposed that they both leave the next day for an "adventure" in Winnipeg.

"After we both arrived safe, we had to find a place to stay. You have to remember that this was a spur of the moment trip and we did not have anything planned. Eventually, we found this affordable motel—actually the place was a dive—but we did not mind. It was all part of the adventure," Jane explained.

Despite their determination to turn the lemon of a motel into lemon meringue pie, the novelty of staying in a rundown place soon wore off. They had to vacate the room they were initially assigned because of a "foul odour [then] on the second day we decided to check out and try and find a more suitable place."

Jane reported that they scoured the city "without much luck." As a result, "we decided it would not hurt if we were to stay in the first motel for one more night. So after we checked in one more time, we went to our room and turned on the heater. The weather outside was horrible. There was a blizzard ... [it was] freezing cold, with many feet of snow and ice. As we were on a budget and travelling by foot, we decided to walk to the Safeway store that was a short distance away, to stock up on food. We decided that this was cheaper than going to restaurants. We thought that by the time we returned to the room, it would be very cozy and warm. [After] about an hour and a half, we returned, frozen to the bone only to find our room freezing cold."

In her re-telling of the incident, Jane stressed the temperature situation by explaining, "I mean, it was warmer outside than it was in our room. So we called the front desk and they came to check it out. They could not find anything wrong but in the end moved us to another room.

"Now that we were settled in our new room we were both drained from the day and went to sleep early. It was not very dark [in the room] when we went to sleep. You could still see everything in the room clearly. Suddenly, we both heard the sound of someone walking on the carpet in our room. Now these rooms were not very big, all they had was a bed, a desk and a washroom, so with one glimpse you could see the whole room. After the footsteps someone or something sat on the bed. We both felt it. We were too scared to say anything and we both lay rigid as boards until sleep took over. We did not discuss these events with each other until the next day as we were checking out for good."

By now, anxious to throw regard for their budget to the wind, the two women "settled into another hotel across the road." Jane's boyfriend paid them a call and it was only then that they finally discussed the strange experiences in the motel.

"Apparently, a few years ago there was a major fight that took place in that motel. It started in the room with no heat and then moved next door to the room with the invisible walker. One of the individuals who was in that fight was killed in there and it was a gruesome sight ... blood covered the walls and carpet."

At least now the women had some sort of an explanation as to why the rooms in what seemed to be a decrepit, nondescript motel, displayed decidedly eerie qualities—qualities, such as foul odours, lack of heat and phantom footsteps, that are usually associated with a ghostly presence.

Jane allowed that she was glad she hadn't known the history of the rooms she and her friends stayed in while they were in Winnipeg, although she also acknowledged that on some level she must have known there was something very wrong with the place. Given her long-standing background of living in a haunted house, the frequency and necessity of the room changes for such different reasons would have been enough of a clue.

And so, Jane left the haunted motel in Winnipeg behind and returned to her haunted house in Calgary.

George and the Manitoba Theatre Centre

MTC, the Manitoba Theatre Centre, is a dynamic and unique institution that dates back some forty years and has developed a large and loyal following. So loyal, in fact, that when the company moved from its original home in the Dominion Theatre, everyone—staff, patrons and resident ghost—went along to the new venue.

"I've never seen him," Teena Laird, long-time MTC employee, remarked recently. "I feel his presence. Others have seen him though."

Perhaps because he has actually been sighted, the theatre staff is convinced that the ghost is George, the adolescent son of a former caretaker at the Dominion. George and his father lived in rooms above the theatre. The boy used a wheelchair to get around and when a fire broke out in the theatre building the poor lad was trapped. He died in the fire.

Legend has it that during his short existence, George enjoyed an intense passion for the theatre and longed for a career on stage. The depth of the boy's longing must have been profound for, to this day, George's spirit haunts the Manitoba Theatre Centre.

For the first couple of years after the company moved its current location, they presumed they had left George behind.

Then one day it became obvious that the spirit was back among the living.

"It was like he was searching for us. It took a while for him to come here. It didn't happen in the first year."

The staff was glad to have the youngster's spirit back in their midst again.

"He's friendly, he won't harm you, but he's mischievous just like a boy his age might be," explained Teena before specifying, "Things will disappear for a time and then after you've been searching for it and you get exasperated, there it will be, right by your hand. Filing can be difficult with George around. He'll take the very file you need and it will disappear. You just can't find it for a while. Then it just shows up."

George once joined a group of theatre employees during an impromptu social break.

"[We] were socializing, just chatting, and all of a sudden a calculator started working. It was like there'd been a power surge except that it kept on working. It was like he was trying to join our conversation," the personable Ms. Laird recalled.

George's choice to use an electrically connected source is not surprising. Those in the spirit world are clearly drawn to things electrical and electronic. There is a widely held theory that a ghost is the essence or energy left behind after death. If this theory is correct then its attraction to external sources of energy is most understandable.

George did not make an appearance to the group that day, but Peter Wingate, a theatre designer originally from New York, sees the spirit occasionally when he's been working late at night, alone in the theatre. Wingate apparently accepts George's presence as being one of the benefits of his association with the theatre.

Even Wingate's commendably accepting attitude might have been jostled a little had he witnessed George's stunt with the theatre seats. Teena remembered the day when MTC was still

As a child, George lived in the Dominion Theatre with his father.

located in the Dominion Theatre: "All the seats were down … and [then] it was like someone was running down the rows, flipping the seats up."

Teena's curiosity was undeniably piqued. She actually crawled under the seats to search for a clue as to what might have caused such an anomaly. Of course, there was nothing anywhere to be found—nothing that could be seen, that is.

By now George is as much a part of MTC as are stellar performances. Teena explained that, while others might find the behaviour odd, she and other staff members make a point of talking to George throughout the day. When a new person joins the staff at the Manitoba Theatre Centre, they're often skeptical and find the staff's comments to an invisible being amusing. That attitude of disbelief usually doesn't last too long, however. Once they have witnessed a ghostly prank or two, their skepticism quickly dissolves.

By way of justification for her determined stance, Teena described a time when she needed to find two particular receipts. The situation was similar to finding the proverbial "needle in the haystack" and yet it was very important that the documents be found. Teena knew whom she had to call on for help, and moments after making that request the receipts fluttered into an otherwise empty wastepaper basket.

All of this is not meant to imply that George is any kind of a saintly ghost. He took a dislike to a certain actor and made the man's life miserable. Another time George interfered with a stage set by throwing books, which were being used as props, off the shelves where they'd been placed.

Despite all proof to the contrary, not everyone believes in George's existence. Drama professor Reg Skene acknowledges that there is a long-standing tradition of ghosts in theatres. "Every theatre needs a ghost," he once told a reporter. He then went on to suggest that as the new MTC quarters had not had time to acquire a ghost, the staff merely "imported" one from its previous venue.

For Teena, however, who works in the theatre on a daily basis, that theme isn't even worthy of entertaining.

"We believe in this very strongly," she stated emphatically. "I feel him all the time."

Given Teena Laird's long and respected association with the Manitoba Theatre Centre, as well as the verification she offers from others, it seems to me that it would be rude to walk into the theatre without at least acknowledging George's presence.

Mother Tucker's Ghost

The list of ghostly stunts that have been performed over the years at 335 Donald Street in Winnipeg is almost infinite. The list of potential candidates for whom the ghost might be is somewhat more limited.

The building that now houses Mother Tucker's Restaurant was constructed in 1895 as a Masonic Temple. To me, it seems very likely that the building's resident ghost is a former Mason who has somehow never completely left his beloved meeting hall. The Masons are a worldwide fraternal organization with a history that, some say, can be traced back to the Druids. Others might dispute such a claim, but all recognize that the tradition of the Masonic Order goes back at least to the eleventh century.

In its earliest incarnation the organization was really a forerunner to today's trade unions. Stone masons, travelling from town to town building churches, drew together for the purpose of protecting one another's rights and trade secrets. The secretive aspect of the group has been retained, and it is probably this secrecy that has caused them the most trouble over the years. Masons have been, at different times and places, hated, revered, feared and even accused of mortal crimes. With this long and colourful heritage, the Masonic Order moved into Canada in 1875. Manitoba was the seventh province to welcome a chapter of Masons to its roster of organizations, and the building on Donald Street was, at the time of its construction, considered virtually a flagship temple.

Over the years, thousands of Masons came and went through the doors on Donald Street. Year after year, rituals, which are taken extremely seriously by the group's members, were completed over and over again. It would be difficult to conjure up a more effective way than that to create a psychic imprint on a building's atmosphere. And that's exactly what happened. The essence of what and who went before has apparently been indelibly etched in the environment. In other words, the building is haunted, most likely by the ghost of a Mason. Through some of his ghostly hijinks, we can even pinpoint at least one year this particular Mason was active in the fraternity.

"In this year of 1919," a disembodied male voice was heard saying into a telephone receiver. The point of concern here was that the calendar on the wall at Mother Tucker's restaurant confirmed what the employee who'd overheard the comment knew full well—the year was actually 1975.

As eerie as that particular anecdote is, it is completely in keeping with the expected qualities of a true ghost story. Phantoms are almost always attracted to sources of energy. They thrive on proximity to all sorts of receivers and transmitters. The telephone, because it not only does both but is electrically powered, is often one of a ghost's methods of communication.

Many of the other strange goings-on around the restaurant over the years lend credence to the power-base theory of manifestation. One evening when all else was normal, most of the electrical appliances in the place took turns becoming dysfunctional. The cash register, the dishwasher and the ice machine all stopped running and then all re-started for no apparent reason.

The ghost also frequently manipulates the building's lighting system by randomly turning the lights off and on. Occasionally at night the switchboard will light up completely even though there are no incoming calls. The burglar alarm has been similarly affected, ringing when there were no intruders.

A former Masonic Temple, Mother Tucker's is a popular haunted restaurant.

When the building is quiet, phantom footsteps can be heard walking across a lower floor. An employee who heard the distinctive sounds of someone walking, where no one should have been at that time, dutifully went to investigate. There was no one there. No one that he could see, anyway. The man was so convinced that he'd been witness to unseen ghostly movement and was so upset by the thought that he handed in his resignation just before scurrying out of the restaurant as quickly as his frightened legs would carry him.

Other employees have demonstrated a much calmer nature, for instance the worker who stood and stared in amazement as a white figure made its way down a staircase. He remained employed as did another member of the Mother Tucker's kitchen staff. This second employee didn't have the advantage of hearing footsteps before he turned around to find himself face to face with a mustached man whose hair was neatly parted in the middle. The vision was attired as though from a previous era.

The startled cook stared in disbelief as the apparition turned and ascended the stairs leading to the building's attic. He rounded up some of his colleagues and together the group trekked upstairs. No one was there despite the fact that the cook was adamantly certain of what he'd seen and equally certain that no one had come back down the only possible staircase.

What they did find in the topmost storage area was almost more provocative than if they had actually spotted the apparition. There, on the attic floor, lay a tiny, green coffin. Thankfully for the nervous systems of those gathered on the top floor, it was clear that the coffin had never been used. It contained an appropriately sized mattress and an equally small pillow as well as a peculiarly shaped cap. Not surprisingly, everyone was rather flustered by the discovery. After all, they all knew that the building had once been a Masonic Hall and was now a restaurant. By no stretch of the imagination could anyone present determine why a child's coffin would have been brought into the building.

To date, that rather gruesome riddle has not been solved but even if it had been it probably wouldn't have done much to explain the haunting anyway. Enough people have seen and/or heard the ghost at Mother Tucker's for us to know that the resident presence is an adult male—not a small child.

Manager Carlos Ferreira, an admitted skeptic, is nonetheless tolerant of all the interest in his restaurant's status as a haunted building. By now he's almost come to expect visits and phone calls from the media around Halloween time.

"One Halloween a local radio station did their morning show from here after spending the night," he explained by way of citing a recent example. Nothing out of the ordinary occurred during the pre-arranged pyjama party, which is really quite surprising considering spirits are often drawn to radio transmission equipment. (It's not unusual for radio stations to be homes to ghosts.) The psychic they brought in, however, reported she was able to sense a presence.

I asked if the visiting medium had given any indication as to whether the spirit could be a former Mason. Ferreira replied, "She didn't go into that much detail but did say that the person was comfortable here and happy, that he liked the atmosphere and all the people."

Considering his intense interest in running a top-quality restaurant and his decided disinterest in ghosts, this information was the most important Ferreira had ever received about the supernatural presence that many believe inhabits Mother Tucker's. He said, "He [the ghost] had better like [the people here], after all this is a bar and restaurant," alluding to the fact that either a misanthrope "ghost or person would not be too happy with all the action around here. There's always lots of comings and goings so everyone associated with the restaurant needs to be a people person—even the ghosts."

The radio station's lack of success in meeting the phantom isn't too surprising considering the spirit's history of residency in the charming old building. Some years his presence is barely noted although Ferreira did concede "... over the years I have had staff who have not been too comfortable in certain parts of the building alone." Other years there's been a lot of paranormal evidence.

"One employee said he saw a person in the dining room and another said he saw a man in the basement," the manager recalled. To a believer that is pretty stiff evidence. Ferreira, however, would need to see something for himself before he believed it. "I've [worked] here since 1982 and I've never seen or experienced anything [out of the ordinary]."

He was, however, happy to relate, "the latest incident. About a year ago there was a customer having dinner with members of her family. She took pictures of [her brother-in-law in front of] one of our buffets. There was a mirror over the buffet and when the pictures were developed one showed a blurred face in the mirror.

The television and radio stations got a hold of [that information] and they were right over here. A cameraman, in preparation to set up, was taking some Polaroid shots of the place. He took some of the buffet. Some people said those shots also showed a blurred image of a face in the mirror."

In keeping with Ferreira's skeptical nature, he pronounced that seeing such an image "would take a pretty good stretch." Despite his disbelief, many others objectively assessed that there was a face in the photographs that had not been visible to the naked eye when the shots were taken.

When the phantom of the restaurant is not busy allowing himself to be photographed, he is busy with his poltergeist-like activities. Sometimes the locks on the doors inside the building will lock and then unlock at times when no one has been near them with a key. Whoever he is, the ghost must realize by now that he is in a restaurant, for occasionally he lines table napkins and cutlery up in a row before leaving them for unsuspecting staff members to find. The ghost has also been blamed for upsetting prepared dinner tables. One person swears she watched as a disembodied pair of green eyes floated about the room. Another maintains the apparition appeared as an old man dressed all in white. Such a sighting at Mother Tucker's must have caused concern about the possibility of Colonel Saunders looking around for a new "secret recipe"—this one for beef rather than chicken.

Although the ghost in this downtown restaurant displays many classic ghostly characteristics, one of his stunts was considerably more impressive than all the others. Because of the ghost's fondness for telephone tampering, repair workers from the telephone company have had to visit the restaurant frequently over the years. Some of them have even had the unnerving experience of having to work while being watched by unseen eyes.

It was in 1975, however, that the phantom performed his most amazing telephone trick. The telephone company's representatives were called in because none of the phones in the building were working. Upon checking the incoming lines, the repairman could clearly see why there was no phone service to the building. The lines had been cut straight through. The job was a neat one, especially considering the difficulty of the task—the cut occurred beneath several metres of cement! Over the years I've heard and read many, many ghost stories but that chronicle even surprised me.

And so, as always, the choice of whether to believe in the presence of spirits or not is yours. While researching any ghost story, I try to investigate as many points of view as possible. In checking out this story, I felt that I had travelled the length of the belief/disbelief continuum. First, I spoke with Carlos Ferreira, the skeptical manager who feels the most mysterious aspect to the whole thing is how it could all have gotten started. My next call was to psychic Shelley O'Day who has distinctly felt spirits in the restaurant. Personally, given the sheer bulk of other evidence, I'm afraid I'd have to side with Miss O'Day and hope that Mr. Ferreira will still find me a good table in his restaurant—one that is within sight of one of the many places its resident ghost has been seen.

Boys Spooked by Ghost

Boys with time on their hands are usually pretty ingenious about getting into mischief. Dennis Rogers, his brother and their friends were certainly no exception. In time-honoured boyhood tradition, if a good time didn't find them—they found it.

There was, however, one way in which Dennis Rogers was different from the others. You see, he knew, even by his early teens, that he was considerably more psychically sensitive than most people—certainly more sensitive than most of his peers. Perhaps, more importantly, he understood the implications that this gift of insight carried with it.

Dennis occasionally had meaningful dreams; they were dreams that woke him in a sudden shock and were coupled with frustrating amnesia that meant he could not—upon wakening—remember what it was he'd dreamed about. He could not bring to his conscious mind anything about the dream, until almost the very instant that information became important.

Dennis explained that inevitably, three months to "the day" after such a dream, some seemingly random event would occur to trigger total and instant recall of that forgotten reverie.

"I know something a split second before it happens," he revealed, before offering the following example as a dramatic explanation.

In the mid-1970s, Dennis and his friend were swimming at the newly constructed Pan Am Pool in Thompson.

"There's a chrome railing with steps on either side. I was about

15 feet away and my friend Darryl was sitting on the railing. He was [getting ready to] slide into the water. He said something—he said one thing," Dennis repeated for emphasis. "I realized 'I've heard this before' and I ran [to Darryl]. I dove [towards him] just as he flipped over backwards. He would've hit his head on the corner of the concrete. Where my hand caught him would've been the small of his neck. I've still got a mark on my hand from that."

Once they'd both calmed down, Dennis realized where he'd first heard the words that triggered his swift and probably life-saving action. It had been three months before in his vivid, but at the time, forgotten, dream. He'd dreamed the entire sequence of events three months before they occurred and that subconscious knowledge allowed him to prevent a terrible tragedy.

Dennis's gift didn't always manifest itself quite that profoundly. When he and a friend decided to collect empty bottles as a way of financing their admission to a movie, Dennis was inexplicably drawn to a particular corner of a particular building. There, he found an empty beer bottle with a twenty-dollar bill stuffed inside. His hunch had led them directly to more than enough money for not only their movie tickets but once inside, all the treats their teenaged stomachs could hold. Even better, the find had saved them hours of searching for the number of empties necessary to finance their recreation.

Oddly, when Dennis saw a ghost, this extreme sensitivity of his probably didn't play much of a role. He was with close friends, people he knew well; well enough to know they did not share his psychic abilities. They all, however, shared the ghost sighting.

"There were five of us involved in this. We were all teenagers, except for my brother and he was either eleven or twelve at the time. The rest of us were between the ages of thirteen and fifteen. We used to go over to a construction [site] and play tag, something you were NOT supposed to do," Dennis explained.

By the time the ghost-sighting took place, the structure of the building was up and the interior walls were in place.

"We had managed to fix the north door, which was a fire exit [so that] we could get in. There was five young people, in the dark, you're giggling, you're horsing around, all this wonderful stuff, eh," Dennis recalled with enthusiasm. "We get in ... and then all of us heard it. It sounded like something being dragged. Of course, we all froze thinking there was someone on the other side [of the door]. We waited, waited, waited and it stopped. So, of course, we all started again with the giggling. We got right up to the door. Light was coming in under the door and the sounds started again. [The dragging sound] came right up to the door itself but there was no shadow [blocking the light shining through under the door] like there should have been, but it was the same dragging sound. We're all frozen, waiting, in case the door opened. Just fixed to run back down the stairs and out, but it never happened. Then the sound started moving away. We waited and waited and finally [the noise] stopped. This whole thing took about twenty minutes," Dennis recalled.

Given their healthy young nervous systems, the boys were soon calm enough to track down the source of the mysterious sound. After a fruitless search, they determined that the building was completely empty aside from the five of them. Not knowing whether they were relieved or disappointed, the group sat down to plan its next move.

"I happened to glance down and this man stepped into a corner—now these are solid concrete walls—he stepped into the corner from a doorway. I made eye contact [with the image]. He stared straight at me. I said or did something that caught [the other boys' attention]. They looked at me [then] they looked and they saw ... the apparition. It did not say a word ... just stepped sideways the opposite way he came in [through] a solid concrete wall. I watched him go right into the wall and ... disappear."

Thoroughly spooked by what they'd just witnessed, Dennis recalled with a chuckle that he and the others "disappeared as fast as [the ghost] did."

Despite the fact that twenty-five years had passed since the day of that sighting, its image is still fresh in Dennis's mind. He remembered that they could not see through the ghost; that the image was solid in appearance; and as apparently solid as the concrete wall it walked into.

"I can even tell you what this guy was wearing, I saw him that clearly. This guy was wearing the old-style bib coveralls, and he had a work shirt on underneath. He had work boots on. Who was he?" Dennis asked rhetorically. "I always pictured those old-style coveralls as being farmer-style but there's no farmland [around Thompson]. The only other thing I can come up with is a trapper, but why would a trapper wear those coveralls and have work boots?"

Nor did the location of the sighting give Dennis any clues. He explained that before construction began on the building where the ghost was seen the area, "was all trees, to my knowledge there had never, ever been a building in that place. The only thing that I could come up with is that this spirit travelled. Beyond that I have no idea," he concluded in a puzzled-sounding voice.

Dennis might well have been on the right track with his presumption that the image had travelled to that spot. If the ghost wasn't connected in any way with either the building or its location, then perhaps the spirit's connection was directly with one or more of the boys who witnessed its appearance. After all, these were youngsters too intent on having fun to realize that they could have been putting their safety in jeopardy. The manifestation might have been the spirit of a concerned ancestor returning to keep an eye on the boys.

We will never know for sure, but Dennis Rogers did add that after this experience, his friends, understandably, stopped playing at the construction site. He did, however, maintain a special interest in the building that has purposely been unidentified in this story. It became a public place which, over the years, has welcomed thousands of people, youngsters and adults alike. Despite this, and Dennis's attention to news of the place, he never heard even as much as a rumour that the building was haunted. This absence of reports seems to lend credence to the theory that the ghost was associated with the trespassing children rather than the venue itself.

Hotel Has Permanent Guests

Opulent, luxurious, stately, elegant. The Hotel Fort Garry has, correctly, been called all of the above. There is, however, another equally descriptive and accurate word that could apply to the grand old lady of Winnipeg's hospitality industry. That word is "haunted." Hotel Fort Garry is well and truly haunted.

That fact, in itself, is really not too surprising. Many hotels all over the world are home to ghosts. It is, however, somewhat unusual for a Canadian hotel to be so honest about its haunted status. While the British could hardly conceive of a hotel without at least one ghost, we in the colonies are, often, more hesitant to acknowledge our supernatural visitors.

This hesitancy is certainly not evident with the staff at Hotel Fort Garry. Assistant Manager Don Klassen opened a conversation about the hotel's ghosts with the following statements: "Ah, yes, our ghosts. If you have access to the Internet, you can find them on our web page." Spirits receiving recognition in cyberspace—surely that must absolutely define a modern-day ghost hunter's dream come true.

To understand the origin of Hotel Fort Garry's ghost stories, however, we need to harken back to a time long before anyone had ever even heard of computers—an earlier, more refined time, specifically the bitterly cold evening of December 10, 1913, the night of the hotel's official opening, which was celebrated with a gala ball. It was fully two years after the first shovel dug into the ground to begin excavation for the enormous construction project that the nine-storey hotel at Broadway and Main was ready to receive its first guests.

The write-up in the following day's edition of the *Free Press* went on for two pages under a headline that referred to the dance: "FUNCTION OF GREAT BRILLIANCY." Of course, as none of us were there, it would be hard to argue the accuracy of the description but the word choice does seem a trifle strange by today's standards.

The article that followed gushed not only about the splendour of the hotel, but also about the dancers and their apparel, specifically the women's gowns. No accurate census remains as to how many people attended the ball, but the reporter did explain, "It would take hours to describe the lovely gowns made so much lovelier against the handsome background of the gorgeous rooms and hangings but a *few* [emphasis mine] noticed were those worn by. ..." The reporter then listed 104 women's names followed by a description of their dresses. The details revealed in those descriptions varied in length from, "Mrs. Cameron who wore a beautiful gown of violet charmeuse with tunic and bodice of black and white lace and a sash end in front of the charmeuse" to "Mrs. Lorne Cosby, yellow satin charmeuse." In keeping with the custom of the day, few of the women were referred to by their given names but rather were variously identified as (for instance) Mrs. Myers or Miss Thomson or Mrs. F.H. Brydges or Mrs. J.C. Waugh or Mrs. Nicholas Bawlf.

Their lack of individual identity apparently didn't have any dampening effect on the ladies' enjoyment of the ball, however, as they danced the night away on a "perfect floor" under "magnificent crystal chandeliers." One of those ladies might even have had such a good time at the party that, after death, she chose to return there and celebrate into eternity.

Present-day staff first became aware of the lady's spirit when a guest returned to the hotel after having stayed there on other occasions. Assistant Manager Klassen was working on the front desk when the woman arrived. She requested a specific room. That in itself wasn't too unusual but Klassen felt compelled to tell her that on that particular day there were more desirable rooms available. He explained to her that the room she had requested didn't afford much of a view and that he could book her into a room that he thought she would enjoy more.

Despite Klassen's explanation, the woman stood her ground. She wanted to stay in the room she'd been assigned before because, she told the assistant manager, "The spirits visit me there."

Perplexed, Klassen probed, "Spirits?"

Warming to the man's interest, the visitor explained that she regularly saw an image in that room—an image of a woman in a ball gown.

"She hovers at the foot of my bed and after that she moves out the window," the guest recounted.

Of course, Klassen agreed to rent the woman the room that she had requested, but the brief conversation did get him wondering. He had no idea who the apparition might have been in life or why she was staying around to haunt the hotel. It wasn't until Klassen

The historic Fort Garry Hotel—home to ghosts.

had related the incident to a reporter who checked the newspaper's archives and discovered the write-up about the grand opening festivities, that the man had any clue as to the origin of the apparition. After reading the long-winded description, he wondered if the ghost was someone who'd attended the party.

While agreeing that Klassen's theory might be the correct one, there's also the possibility that the ghost is a Cinderella-like spirit—the essence of a woman who wanted desperately to go to the ball and wasn't able to. Lacking the necessary magic of a fairy godmother during her life, the lady might have simply chosen to party into eternity.

That particular spirit will certainly not be lonely while she awaits the arrival of her prince at the ball. There are clearly others at the hotel sharing the mysterious dimension she inhabits—the phantom diner, for instance. Like his association with the lady in the ball gown, Klassen's encounter with the spirit of the man in the dining room was only an indirect one. Still, he recalled the incident clearly. It occurred in 1989 during the wee hours of a graveyard shirt. All in the hotel was as quiet as he had expected it would have been. Klassen was taking advantage of the tranquillity by attending to routine paperwork. Suddenly, a kitchen employee came hurrying into the office area looking for him. It seems the man had been washing dishes with another employee when they heard sounds coming from the hotel's dining room. As the dishwashers were sure they were the only two in that area of the hotel, they immediately went to investigate. That's when they saw him—the man sitting at a table in the dining room, cutlery in hand, enjoying a meal. The men stared in horror and fascination as the apparition continued to eat, completely oblivious to his audience.

The employees knew there was something very wrong with the scenario that had unfolded before them, but they didn't have any idea what they were dealing with. Was this a hotel guest who'd somehow been left behind from that night's dinner? Or did the image's origin date back considerably before present time? Whichever the case might have been, they clearly felt they needed someone in authority with them and so they ran for the assistant manager. By the time the trio made its way back to the dining room, it was as empty as it should have been.

Could they possibly have had a late-night diner? they wondered, but ruled the possibility out after determining that all the doors remained locked—from the inside. It seemed there had been no trespasser, not from this dimension anyway, and there was no evidence of it, because by now the image had faded.

That occurrence in the dining room area was not a completely isolated event. Other staff members have reported hearing the sounds of dishes clattering late at night when they know there is no one in that section of the hotel.

But poltergeists rattling dishes, apparitions dining and images in ball gowns are not the only mysteries at Hotel Fort Garry. It is even home to a rather rare paranormal phenomenon: a "ghost light." This apparently sourceless light has been seen moving through the hallways on more than one occasion.

At least one of the hotel's spirits has been bold enough to make its presence known to manager Ida Albo. The normally down-to-earth woman is convinced that she had a close encounter with a spirit in her private hotel suite. She had gone to bed ahead of her husband one night and had immediately fallen into a deep sleep. Sometime later she heard what she presumed was her husband coming into the room. Those sounds were followed by the distinct feeling of someone sitting on the bed beside her. Wondering why her husband would sit down beside her instead of just coming to bed as he normally would have, she rolled over to ask him why he was there. Despite knowing with certainty what she'd heard and what she'd felt, Ida Albo found herself staring around a completely empty room.

Perhaps that first-hand experience convinced the manager of her hotel's haunted status for she was delighted when actor Bill Murray, previously of *Ghost Busters* fame, dropped in for a visit. Unfortunately, if the movie star had any paranormal experiences during his stay they have, thus far, gone unrecorded. Perhaps, we will have to wait and see if Winnipeg's opulent, luxurious, stately, elegant and very haunted hotel turns up as the backdrop for a movie. Until then, we can just enjoy the fact that Manitoba is home to a supernaturally outstanding hotel.

Archives Collections Include Ghosts

After collecting dozens of Manitoba ghost stories, I decided it was time to start looking for photographs to go with a few of the spooky tales. Towards this end, I telephoned the Manitoba Provincial Archives and left a request for the photo archivist to give me a call. Not long after, Lynne Champagne returned my call and within minutes we were able to arrange a system whereby I would be able to chose the most appropriate pictures to complement the text.

Once the business had been transacted, Lynne and I chatted briefly and she expressed interest in my project. Most people greet the news that someone is doing something as off-the-wall as collecting and compiling local ghost stories with at least mild interest. Occasionally, though, I do get strongly negative responses so I'm always a bit on guard when people ask questions. Because of this, I gave Lynne a brief explanation and then paused. That pause was met with one of equal length on the other end of the line. Just for a moment I thought, *Oh no, she's not going to react well.*

Thankfully, my fears were completely groundless for when Lynne replied seconds later, her voice did not in any way reflect a negative attitude; she merely sounded puzzled and inquired as to whether or not I would be interested in including the story about the ghosts in the Archives building. I could hardly believe my good fortune. In one call I was not only able to arrange for the necessary photographs but also to add a wonderful story to my cache.

Judging by its history, the building that houses Manitoba's Provincial Archives certainly has every right to be haunted. It was constructed in the 1930s as one of the Depression-related make-work projects. The building was originally designed as Winnipeg's Civic Auditorium, a function it served for nearly four decades.

Over the years, dozens of world-class entertainers played to packed houses here, even during the lowest days of the Great Depression. It was a time when many Winnipeg citizens had legitimate concerns about where their next meal might be coming from. Despite the harsh financial conditions, Winnipeg's Civic Auditorium successfully hosted such internationally renowned performers as Lily Pons, Vladimir Horowitz, Lawrence Tibbett, Marion Anderson, Paul Robeson and others. This in itself was an amazing feat when you consider that times were so tough that many New York theatres were dark—closed, waiting out the end of the Depression. But the Civic Auditorium was not just booking these performances, it was consistently selling out the shows. The stars were playing to full, and most appreciative, houses, night after night.

My experience in collecting ghost stories has taught me that such an emotionally charged environment is ripe for a future haunting. Musicians, actors and other performers, who tend to be highly emotional folk anyway, are straining to project those emotions to a large group of people. And that same group, having committed to temporarily being an audience, have intentionally made themselves as receptive as possible. The exchange of energy under such circumstances is profound.

One widely accepted theory that attempts to explain the existence of spirits in our world proposes that spirits are a form of "leftover energy." If this is so, then the potential for an entertainment hall to become haunted is obvious and from what Lynne described, it sounds as though this is exactly what has happened with what is now the Archives building.

"The security guards who work here overnight tell us that the motion sensors in the main reading room frequently go off even though they [the guards] can see that there is no one in the room at the time," Lynne began.

She recalled that one guard, a man who has since retired, found an effective way of dealing with his invisible companions. If the ghosts were exceptionally active, setting off the sensors frequently, he "would tell the ghost to 'shut up' and then things would be quiet for a while."

But the phantoms' activities were not restricted to involvement with the night-time staff.

"People would come in to work and find all their stuff taped to their desk. Pens, papers, everything they'd left out would be taped down when they came to work in the morning," Lynne explained, before adding that she arrives at the building well before most of the other office staff. "When I come in, I hear what sounds like someone opening and closing doors."

She's become used to the unusual sound effects, though, because, "There's always something banging. It's never anything harmful although one ... employee refused to work here."

Lynne concurred with my theory that an archives, like a museum, has great potential to play host to presences. After all, by definition an archives is a repository for significant records and there are often highly emotional reasons for those records to come into being. The traumatic energy associated with some historical events has simply not dissipated. Combine that with the unique history of the building that houses the Manitoba Provincial Archives and there's really not much wonder that the stately old building is home to a few spirits.

The former Civic Auditorium is now the provincial archives.

And so, if you have occasion to drop in to the Archives building any time in the future, you might just enjoy your visit even more now, knowing you could be sharing space with some of the greatest names in the history of show business.

Chapter 3

LOVED ONES RETURN

Cross Lake Apparition

Certainly some people are far more likely to see a ghost than are others. Those who tend towards sightings simply seem more perceptive of the spirit world—in effect, more tuned to that wavelength, if you will. As a result, some people take ghost-sightings as a natural part of their day-to-day lives, while others of us could go to our graves never having seen or even felt the presence of a ghost.

If some people are more likely to be treated to a glimpse of the world beyond, is the reverse also true? Are some spirits more likely than others to visit earth? In a review of the documentation available, it would appear that the stronger the person's personality was in life, the greater the chance of that person's ghost visiting the living. This concept is especially interesting when you consider that over the years and all around the world, the most frequently seen apparition is that of the Virgin Mary.

Sightings of the Virgin Mary have been reported from all over the world: France, Egypt, the United States and at least twice in Manitoba. These appearances often coincide with the Easter season and so the apparition that was seen at Cross Lake during the last week in March of 1992 is an almost classic example of this phenomenon.

Although the Catholic Church refused to officially comment on the sensation, newspapers as far away as Winnipeg thought the story warranted front page coverage. It seemed that on

Thursday, March 26, 1992, a "hazy image" appeared on Shirley Thomas' front door. Upon closer examination, the woman determined that the image resembled that of the Virgin Mary.

The town was immediately astir with the news and, predictably, it didn't take long for word to spread to neighbouring communities. The news was especially well received in places like Norway House and St. Theresa Point where large percentages of the population are Catholic. Many people decided to drop whatever they were doing and make a pilgrimage to the mysterious image.

According to reports, the faithful were not disappointed. Comments such as "I felt very warm and close to her [Mary]" and "I got a tingling feeling through my hands and arms" were typical responses from people who had been near the apparition. By Sunday, March 30, officials estimated that more than two hundred followers had approached Thomas' door and seen the specter.

Further reports of a "pulsating star" as well as video clips of two stars descending low over the supposedly haunted house on three separate occasions succeeded in enhancing the credibility of the sighting. Council member Ernie Scott had a rather curious reaction to the combination of the odd astrological display and the sudden appearance of the image. He said, "If the pictures of the stars were not associated with the silhouette, I would dismiss them as *just another UFO sighting* [emphasis mine]."

Local police, however, said they were more concerned about the sudden influx of visitors to an area ill-equipped to deal with such an occurrence. Even before the apparently miraculous apparition was noted in provincial newspapers, the image was drawing crowds. Neighbouring bands were hiring planes to fly their members to Cross Lake to see the vision, with an average of two plane loads arriving a day.

Reporter James Ritchie from Thompson explained, "Cross Lake is a town with no tourism and suddenly hundreds of people converged upon the place. There is only one hotel and it only has about a dozen rooms. Within days, the population had swollen at least ten to twenty percent with no way to accommodate the visitors."

Meanwhile, all this attention did nothing to alter the image on the door. Those present with a slightly more scientific bent tried to determine whether or not the image was genuine. People rubbed at it, in an attempt to erase the vision from the door, with no effect. Others blocked all possible light sources to the door, but the image only became brighter. Believers were thoroughly convinced that they were hosting a visit from the spirit of the Virgin Mary.

"I believe it's a sign," Councillor Scott replied when asked his opinion of the paranormal occurrence.

Not too many days later, the once well-defined image faded and with it the intense interest and the crowds. What had it been? Was it a divinely inspired, heaven-sent apparition or was it, as more pragmatic folks have suggested, just the reflection on a front door of a picture hung on the wall inside the house? Perhaps we'll never know for sure, beyond this philosophical comment by James Ritchie: "I don't know that this is a great ghost story. I think it's a great story about what people wanted to see and *needed* to believe."

There was another Manitoba sighting of the Virgin Mary reported eight years before the Cross Lake story broke. This one, however, was not nearly so well attended. It seems that late in the fall of 1984 near Duck Bay, three friends were boating. In the course of their outing, they approached a marshy area where they knew a woman had recently drowned. At that location apparently all three boaters, simultaneously, saw the apparition of the Virgin Mary among the reeds.

As with any reported sightings there are, of course, many factors at work in the foregoing anecdotes. They are, nonetheless, Manitoba's two rather fascinating contributions to the worldwide collection of Virgin Mary sightings.

Charlie Wasn't Ready to Say Good-bye

The Chandlers, whose haunted house story appears on pp. 40–43, were cat-lovers. One particular feline, "Charlie," however, was a particular family favourite.

"He was the only cat I knew that used to go visiting around the neighbourhood and bring his friends home for lunch," older daughter Brett recalled. Sadly, Charlie's wanders through the neighbourhood would eventually bring on the cat's demise, for just shy of his sixth birthday Charlie disappeared. The family was concerned one evening when he failed to follow his normal pattern of coming home by bedtime and the next morning their worst fears were confirmed. Someone had left the beloved pet's mangled collar, identification tags still attached, on their front porch. Charlie had apparently been hit and killed by a car.

The Chandlers mourned deeply. They had even been deprived of the comfort of a body to bury, our standard symbol of a last good-bye.

It was soon evident that Charlie hadn't been ready to say good-bye even if the Chandlers had been allowed the opportunity, for almost immediately they began to hear familiar Charlie-sounds. They'd hear the bell on his collar ringing as an unseen Charlie jumped down out of his favourite chair. And death could not stop the friendly cat's neighbourhood explorations. The side gate in the fence would rattle just as it had when Charlie had regularly made his way over it on his way to visit his friends.

He even attempted to offer his former owners comfort by rubbing up against their legs in classic cat-like fashion.

"You'd be sitting there and feel a cat rubbing against you, but nobody would be there when you bent over to pet it," was how one family member described the experience.

The ghostly cat-activity continued in the Chandler's home for many years. Eventually, the four humans agreed it was time to bring home a new pet. The kitten's arrival marked the beginning of a noticeable decline in Charlie's after-death presence. The family felt him less and less until eventually the remarkable energy that had been Charlie Chandler's spirit faded away, perhaps on to another plane.

"I think he felt that he could leave us now, that we would be okay and he could move on. We hope he is happy wherever he is," Brett, speaking for the whole Chandler family, said.

Skizzy Came Back

The strength of the bond between pets and their owners is a well-known fact. Occasionally, this bond can even survive death. For instance, I have heard a wonderfully heartwarming story about an elderly couple whose cat went missing and presumably died. A few days later, as the couple were preparing to fall asleep for the night, they felt movement on the covers of their bed. They sat up immediately and turned on the light. At first neither could see anything that might have caused the motion that they felt. A second later, however, a series of tiny indentations across the blanket caught their eyes—they were the sort of marks made by a cat's paw prints. Their beloved pet had returned to comfort and be comforted by its former owners.

After that initial episode, the couple were no longer startled by the tiny footsteps on their bed at bedtime. They knew that there was nothing to fear and so allowed themselves to be comforted by the invisible presence. After a couple of weeks, the phantom nocturnals stopped but by then they had served their purpose: the couple had come to accept the loss of their beloved cat.

A woman in Winnipeg wrote to tell me a similar story. By coincidence her name is Kat—Kat Morgan—but her pet was a ferret. The little animal, a female named Skizzy, had an amazing life. She lived to nearly nine years of age despite the fact that for many years she was ill and on medication. Finally, at the end of April in 1994, Kat, with the help of her trusted veterinarian, made the decision that Skizzy's time on earth had come to an end.

"It was the hardest thing I've ever had to do," Kat wrote, before adding that despite the passage of years, "I still feel the quiet."

Kat has also felt the ghost of her former pet. "I was sweeping

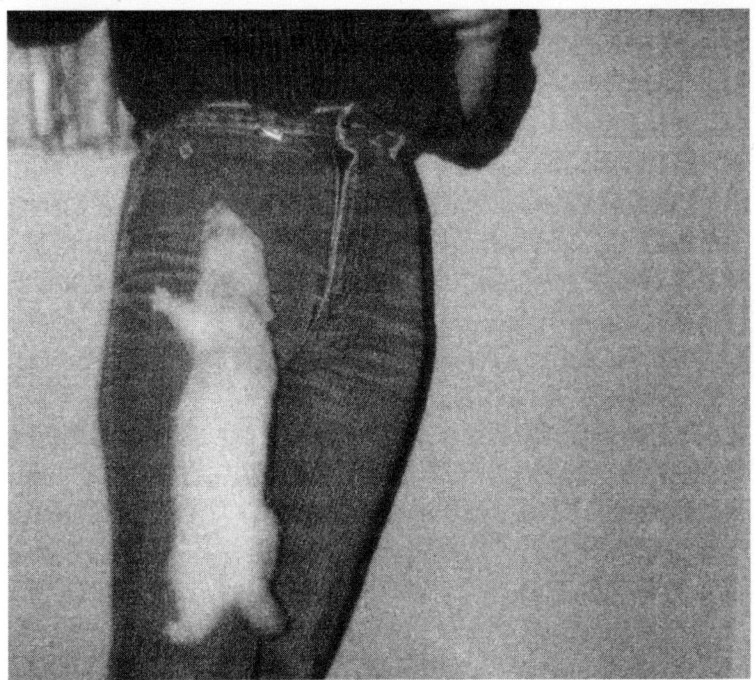

Skizzy, the ferret, in life

the floor and bent down to sweep [the crumbs] into the dust pan and I felt something brush against my ankles. It was Skiz," Kat stated without hesitation.

That particular greeting actually became familiar to Kat as she also felt the little animal brush past her as she stood at the kitchen sink doing dishes.

Skiz made her presence known in other ways as well. Kat frequently caught a sudden whiff of the distinct ferret smell on several occasions when no ferret, at least not one that could be seen, was anywhere around. Another time Skizzy actually made an appearance in the living room mirror at Kat's home. The deceased animal appeared as a "whitish glow about Skizzy's size." The apparition stayed long enough for Kat to check around the room and see if the mirror was reflecting something somewhere in the room. "It was only in the mirror," Kat determined.

And so, even very small animals can now be added to the list of those who have returned after life to visit the people they once lived with.

Old Trevor

The following story originally ran in the Saturday, October 30, 1965, issue of the *Winnipeg Free Press*. Byline credit is given to someone named A.E. Blythe and the story was told in the first person. There is no indication exactly where or when the incident took place but it is, nevertheless, a powerful tale of a man's spirit saving the life of a loved one.

It seems a group of boys, all within that awkward age range that is too old to go out "trick or treating" and yet too young to be completely uninterested by the fact that it was Halloween, headed out to look for a little mischief. "[H]arnessing cows, tipping over outhouses, and blocking gateways with anything movable" were enumerated as some of the activities planned for the evening.

They had not gone very far, for they were still within sight of the school most of them attended. For young Blythe that was apparently not a particularly comforting sight. The stern school master, Milton Trevor, known to the boys by the disparaging nickname, "Old Trevor," boarded with Blythe's family and consequently was able to give the youngster a hard time at home as well as at school. Despite the visual reminder of potential discipline, Blythe kept up with his mates, explaining in the newspaper article that although he was cold and already somewhat spooked by the eeriness of the night, he did not want to be the first to suggest putting an end to the evening's hijinks.

Besides, there was still something of a challenge to be met on that particular Halloween. It seemed that each year, no matter how they varied their route, "Old Trevor" would always catch up with them at some point in the evening and make them re-trace their steps, undoing all the damage they had done. On the year that Blythe was writing about in the *Free Press,* the school teacher had still not apprehended them even though it was long past the time they should have been in their beds.

Although unable to admit they were ready to head for home, Blythe and another boy, Joey, quietly slipped away from the rest of the group. They planned to take a short-cut home. Blythe reported that the pair reached Joey's house without incident and that, at that point, he would only have to cross the river to get to his own home.

The bridge across the river was some distance away but Blythe, in common with every other youngster in town, was familiar with an alternate crossing point—a series of logs, scattered somewhat randomly but stretching from one side of the river to the other. Anxious to be home warm and safe, the boy hurried across the makeshift bridge. He'd made the trip countless times before and even at that speed but the crossing on this dark Halloween night proved to be different—nearly tragically different.

Blythe lost his footing on the wet log. He reported remembering feeling himself fall and he surmised that he must have hit his head and knocked himself out as he went down. From that point on, all Blythe could sense was that he was submerged in icy cold water. After a moment, though, somewhere in the distance, he could hear someone calling his name and urging him to get up. As the child regained consciousness, he opened his eyes and, perhaps for the first time in his young life, he was glad to see "Old Trevor." The dependable teacher, who caught the boys at their pranks every year, had just caught Blythe.

"Go home, boy. Go home, boy," the old man urged the cold, wet and badly frightened Blythe.

Feeling too tired to even make the effort to stand up, but knowing that disobeying the school teacher's direct order would mean being in worse trouble still, Blythe struggled to his feet and made them carry him, step by step, along the path to his house. Trevor, however, did not follow—perhaps he still had to catch up to the other delinquent youngsters.

Fighting to stay conscious and losing strength each step of the way, Blythe dragged himself up to his own front door, his wet clothes heavy and cold against his body. Seconds later, from inside the house, the boy's parents heard a thump and went to investigate. There was their son, in a crumpled heap on the doorstep.

They gathered the lad up and carried him to bed before calling the doctor. Blythe lay in bed fading in and out of consciousness for the next week. His parents kept a constant vigil at his bedside until the periods of consciousness became longer than the periods of unconsciousness. Slowly the child realized that he had been badly hurt when he'd fallen off the log. Then he recalled that it had been the school teacher who had come to his rescue, but that remained a very confusing memory. If "Old Trevor" had been there and seen how badly Blythe had been hurt, why had the man not escorted him home rather than simply ordering him to go?

Over the next few days the boy's strength returned and he was able to sit up in bed and take a little food. After seeing the lad's health steadily improve over the next few days, his mother decided that it was time to let him know of the tragedy that had occurred the night of his near-drowning.

The Blythe family's boarder, local school teacher Milton Trevor, known to the neighbourhood boys as "Old Trevor," had died. The man had succumbed to a sudden heart attack in his room less than an hour before young Blythe had managed to struggle home.

October 31 had clearly been quite a night in the Blythe household, what with the coincidence of Mr. Trevor's death and the youngster's near-fatal accident. Stranger still was that as he lay dying, Milton Trevor had called the boy's name out over and over again.

Blythe concluded his remarkable story with the assurance that he never again went out on Halloween night. He also added that, up to the time of the writing, he remained convinced that it was "Old Trevor" who had come to him as he lay unconscious at the side of the river.

One hopes that, for the rest of his life, A.E. Blythe was able to take comfort from the fact that the unwanted attention he had routinely received from the school master over the years had clearly been motivated by love.

Witness to Murder

In 1909, a gentleman named Mr. Ward was not where he wanted to be. He was away from home, hospitalized in Winnipeg while recovering from major surgery—the amputation of his left leg. Not surprisingly, the man was in a great deal of pain.

Ward had been in touch with his wife and asked that she contact their daughter who was living away from home. Young Louise had recently married a man her parents had never met. The ailing father desperately wanted a visit from his daughter, feeling that her presence would bring him some badly needed comfort.

One morning, just days after the surgery, Ward's pain awakened him. Perhaps Ward himself should pick up the story from this point.

"All of a sudden I was confronted by a vision of a little room, with two struggling occupants. Yes, there was a struggle. I saw it. A man was grappling with my little girl. He had one arm over her shoulder and the other flew at her throat.

"They were standing just in front of a stove. Their bodies swayed in the struggle. Then both drifted out of the room. It didn't seem like they went through a door. It was bigger, maybe not so high, but wider. My little girl seemed to lose her strength and as she dropped her assailant shoved her towards a bed which was in front of him. She lay like senseless. The man ran out into the room which had the stove it. He returned with a club of some kind and dealt her a blow on the head."

Ward's vision was amazingly distinct for he was able to describe his daughter's attacker in great detail.

"He was a man of about 170 pounds. He was about five feet eight inches tall. He wore blue trousers of some kind. They were coated with a white substance as though from laborious work. He had a short blue coat on. I could not see his chin very plainly. My daughter's body hid it from view. His hair was medium in color and straight, and, oh, but I tell you it isn't from what he wore or this that I shall know him. It was the face which planted itself on my memory. Yes, sir, I saw my little girl killed, just as though I stood beside her at the time," he added with a sob.

"I could stand it no longer and attempted to jump out and

grapple with that man. The nurse caught me saying, 'What's the matter?' and my vision was broken. But I saw that man kill her and I will know him the minute I set eyes on him. Yes, I can describe him but beyond the description there was something stronger by which I will know him. It was the expression of his features more than the features themselves. Were he to walk through this corridor now I wouldn't hesitate in picking him out and demanding justice."

Poor Mr. Ward. What a dreadful experience to have had. Any sort of a paranormal encounter is inherently provocative, but to have been a witness from afar to his own daughter's murder must surely have been the manifestation of a parent's worst nightmare.

Aunt Margaret's Farewell

The following story first appeared in the book *Canada's PSI Century,* which was released in 1967 as a centennial project but has long since gone out of print.

The gentleman who submitted this anecdote was identified only as "C.E.P. of Transcona." He begins by advising readers that the incident took place around the turn of the twentieth century, when he was just a boy. C.E.P.'s family consisted of his mother, father, brother and seventy-five-year-old grandfather. They had just finished eating lunch when they clearly heard a knocking on a door leading to another room in the house. These were forceful knocks, he described, not merely tentative rappings.

The story-teller's father got up from the table to open the door but found that there was no one there. "Not visible, anyway" was how C.E.P. put it. Despite the lack of a source for the sound, the boy's grandfather calmly announced, "That was Margaret," referring to his own sister and, coincidentally, last living relative.

Everyone was, of course, very surprised at this announcement for they had no reason to either expect a visit from the great aunt or even to hear from her. She lived some fifty kilometres away and when she had last visited had seemed completely healthy and happy.

A few days later C.E.P and his family were informed that Margaret had died after an illness of only a few days. The time of her death coincided exactly with the sounds of knocking in her nephew's home and her brother's sudden insight.

The Gift of a Rainbow

The next story is also about the power of a relative's love, but this one is as heartwarming as one of the previous ones was distressing.

Spirits can make their presence known in a variety of ways. A distinctive smell is one of the most common methods of communication. A newly widowed woman, for instance, might sense the presence of her recently deceased husband and at the same time detect the smell of the aftershave he always wore. It is considerably less common for a spirit to reveal itself through a particular sight rather than through a scent. The following story, however, describes just such a ghostly spectacle.

The people to whom the following events occurred have asked that their identities be disguised. As the issue is a highly personal one such a request is certainly understandable. I will only confirm that this poignant story took place in Manitoba.

A couple lost their teenaged daughter in a tragic car accident fifteen years before the following incident occurred. To help them cope with their grief, the parents joined a group of other mothers and fathers who had suffered similar losses. The couple found this association so comforting that they maintained their contact with the group long after their day-to-day need for comfort had, blessfully, passed.

One beautiful, cloudless summer's day, they attended an outdoor lunch with this same group of friends. Just before the meeting adjourned, each couple released a balloon into the air to symbolically send greetings to their departed loved one. As the woman released her balloon in memory of her daughter, she wished the girl rainbows.

As the couple got into their car and began the drive home, they noticed a most amazing phenomenon. There, across the otherwise clear sky, was a bright, full rainbow. As they drove the thirty-five or so kilometres home, the rainbow followed them. By the time they'd arrived back at home, the rainbow had become a rare double rainbow.

They knew then that their daughter's spirit had received their greeting and was, in turn, sending her own loving wishes on to them.

Soldier's Cries Heard

This story originally ran in the book *Canada's PSI Century*.

It was a bitterly cold January day in Winnipeg. The year was 1919. A young soldier, back from serving overseas, was shopping for some badly needed civilian clothing. For this reason the young man, who gave his initials as W.J.V., was still wearing his uniform and was therefore readily identifiable as a member of Lord Strathcona's Horse Regiment.

Like all returning soldiers, this young man had been through a lot. He was deeply grateful to have made it home, alive and in one piece. Many of his friends hadn't been so lucky. He'd seen many of them go down in battle and, of course, been profoundly affected by each casualty. There was one young man he remembered especially well—"Frank McK" was how he identified this particular soldier. Frank had been only twenty years old the day W.J.V. had witnessed his death. This tragedy particularly distressed the entire regiment, for Frank had been well-liked by all who knew him.

Trying to put such nightmares as far out of his mind as possible, W.J.V. browsed the racks of suits and casual clothing available in the Eaton's store. As he picked through to find the size he needed, a lad, some years younger than himself, tapped him on the arm. The boy had recognized the uniform. His brother had also been a member of Lord Strathcona's Horse

Regiment, but had not been as fortunate as W.J.V. had been. The boy's older brother—Frank McK—had been killed.

The two spoke for a while before the younger McK extended an invitation to the returning soldier to join Frank's family for a meal. W.J.V. did not want to impose, but the boy assured him the visit would actually bring comfort to his mother and sisters.

The visit was a pleasant one but inevitably the conversation came around to Frank's death. The family asked its guest about the circumstances surrounding the tragedy. As the story unfolded, the family merely nodded knowingly. At first the visitor thought this strange but young Frank's mother soon explained. On the day and at the very time the young man had been killed overseas, his sisters had been preparing a parcel to send to him. Although the mother had not been involved in the process, she suddenly stopped it by saying, "Don't bother packing anything else girls, Frank is gone." Sadly, she was correct, but how could she have known?

Her visitor that evening offered what might have been a partial explanation for her sudden conviction. W.J.V. told the grieving family that in the moments between Frank's injury and his death he had spoken only of his family. Now, W.J.V. had proof that the mental message transmitted from the battlefield moments before his friend's death had been received.

Old Trapper Keeping Watch

Walter Krivda, of The Pas, told me of the following ghostly legend. When he was eighteen, Mr. Krivda said he had happened to overhear the story and it has stayed with him ever since.

Less than one hundred miles due north of The Pas, there was a particularly bountiful trapline. It had been used for many years by a highly skilled native trapper. Inevitably, however, the man became too old to trap and just a little while later, he died. The rights to trap along the old man's line were passed to a younger, equally skilled trapper. For many years the beneficiary carved himself a profitable livelihood out of his inheritance.

Then, one day, much to the younger trapper's surprise, he thought he spotted a sled team off in the distance. He stood and stared in amazement as the trespasser approached, "in a cloud of powdered snow, with a swift team of dogs in harness pulling the sled," according to what Walter heard that day, many years ago. The trapper "called out but got no reply." The interloper was "heavily muffled in a great parka with the hood trimmed in heavy, long fur." His "dogs and toboggan swiftly vanished down the dark woodland road."

The young trapper was justifiably concerned. Was someone poaching from his lines? he wondered. He vowed to make his checks even more frequent and diligent than they usually were. If he suspected even one pelt had been illegally lifted, he would set out in search of the brazen thief. Despite his increased vigilance, the man never saw anything to make him suspicious that someone had robbed him. Eventually, he forgot about the strange sight and the perceived threat.

One winter's evening after attending to his traps all day, the trapper settled down to fix himself a meal of bannock and beaver meat. The night was clear and quiet.

"Suddenly, there was a great stillness and a cold gust seemed to surround him," Walter continued. "He could see in the distance a dog team approaching with the driver standing and waving his whip. In a flash, it was upon him. The flying powdered snow had almost obliterated from view the team and driver. He was gone, as suddenly as he came."

The young trapper stared in disbelief. The driver and team had passed by him at such a speed that he didn't know whether to worry for his traplines or about the supernatural speed he'd just witnessed. When he recovered from the shock, the trapper's concern once again focused on his lines.

"More than ever [he was] convinced ... that a poacher was surely on his trapline," Walter explained. Or could the second dog sled driver even be correctly referred to as a "poacher" for no animals were ever missing from the rightful trapper's lines. The mystery provoked the man but as the years passed without any further incidents of trespassing, the strange team and driver slipped from the forefront of his mind.

One frigid winter's night the trapper made his way back to his home camp. It had been a difficult trip for, in addition to the extreme cold, his sled was heavy with pelts. By now, though, he was close to his destination and so the burden of the exertion lifted, replaced by joy at the bounty of his catch. Looking ahead, towards his camp, he was astonished to see another team and driver approaching "in a great swirl of powdered snow."

Even though it had been years since he'd seen the strange team and driver, he clearly remembered his suspicions about the other man and intended to get a good look at him this time. If both teams maintained their courses, they would draw parallel to each other in a matter of minutes. It would be his chance to identify the man who was posing a threat to his livelihood.

The two men came closer and closer together until they were within feet of one another. As though on cue, the stranger turned his head towards the trapper and smiled. It was the old trapper, the man whose lines he had inherited. This man was no poacher—he was an apparition—a ghost. The spirit of the old man had come back to his old trapline periodically over the years to check on his younger counterpart.

As the younger man stood still in utter amazement, he realized that he could have solved this mystery for himself at the first sighting and spared himself years of fretting. It was clear that the man and his dogs were phantoms—they had left no tracks in the snow.

Unknown Sister, Lifelong Protector

The next story was sent to me some years ago in the form of a detailed letter. Not only is it a heartwarming story but it is also somewhat unique in that it is a highly personal family anecdote while at the same time being an interprovincial ghost story. In order to preserve the "flavour" of the original telling, it is reprinted here as it appeared in George Wood's letter to me.

My father was a railroader—not given to contemplating "the number of angels that could dance on the head of a pin," a practical man, matter-of-fact—a man as sane as a hammer!

He left school at fourteen, having lost a year in bed to rheumatic fever. He went immediately to work. Life was tough. Making a living was not easy and left little time for philosophizing.

Here, then is a story he told me when I was sixteen or seventeen and finishing high school. It amazed me, for I had never seen this dimension of the man.

He worked for the old Grand Trunk Western railway (GTW). After five years on the job he received his first pass. This [pass] entitled him to free passage anywhere in western Canada where the GTW had track.

When his holiday time rolled around, he decided to travel from his home in Portage La Prairie to Edmonton, Alberta where his mother's sister lived with her family. He had no intention of staying with them but promised his mother he would "look in." When he made his visit, Aunt Louise would hear of no other arrangement than that he stay with them.

The family regarded Aunt Louise as somewhat "strange" as she was known to have more than a passing interest in spiritualism and the occult. He slept there and took his meals with the family but beyond that chose to make himself scarce; [he was] busy with what any young man of nineteen or twenty might do—seeing the sights of the "big city." What sights and how big the city might be judged by knowing that this would have been about 1912 or 1913.

At the evening meal a day or two before he was to leave, Aunt Louise announced that she was to have a seance the next evening. Although she'd never met the person, it delighted her to report that "one of the country's leading mediums" was to preside. She had been disturbed to learn that one of the eight guests invited to participate would be unable to attend.

"Jack, I wonder, would you care to sit in?" she asked.

He was caught, lost for any kind of plausible excuse.

As the group sat down to the table, the medium announced that he sensed the presence of an "unbeliever." Dad in his turn sensed who he meant. He regarded the entire event as a fraud.

The medium then turned to him.

"Jack, do you know a little girl named Mary?"

"No," Jack replied.

"That's strange. She's standing behind your chair and says she has a message for you. She says she wants you to know that she is your guardian angel and that you are not to worry about accidents at work. She will protect you from all harm."

The medium then went on to describe her appearance. She was blue-eyed, her hair, which was dark, she wore combed straight back and it fell to her waist. In it was a ribbon holding it in place and matching her dress, which was [made of] white material with purple violets and hung to mid-calf. She wore white stockings and black patent leather shoes. Her age, the psychic judged, to be "about eight years."

My father remained skeptical and did his best to put the whole evening out of his mind. Nothing he had heard made any sense at all.

He arrived back at home [in Portage La Prairie] near supper hour and as the family gathered about the table everyone wanted to know about his holiday, about Aunt Louise and her family. He, quite naturally, related the story of the seance.

When recreating the scene for me, Dad said that his parents were visibly shaken, so much so that they could not continue their meal. Later that evening having regained her composure, my grandmother revealed the reason for their agitation. Mary was their first-born child.

She had died of diphtheria before their second child was a year old. They had decided not to tell the other children until they were "of an age" and later "not to tell them at all." The apparel, as described, was exactly that in which Mary had been buried, accurate to the most minute detail.

How could anyone have known? Aunt Louise knew of the death, of course, but had not attended the funeral and would not therefore have known of the clothing. Grandmother had not revealed those details in any of the infrequent correspondences that passed between the two families. It would be highly unlikely as well that Aunt Louise would have shared any such personal family information with a man she was meeting for the first time. Mary had been eight at the time of her death.

My father told me this story, but never mentioned it to my older brother or sisters. That, he left to me. They were incredulous. When had he chose me? Did he perceive in me a more accepting sensibility? Had he come over the years to accept his "guardian angel?" I am left with these questions.

Retiring after nearly fifty years of railroading and despite many a close call, some in which others were gravely injured, he never had an accident. His sister Mary did her job well.

And so, there you have it—proof that sometimes we have to travel to discover what we have right here at home!

Uncle Wally Returns

In an attempt to gather ghost stories, I contacted editors of dozens of weekly newspapers in towns throughout Manitoba. Oddly, one of these contacts was to the *Selkirk Journal*, which elicited this ghost story from Winnipeg.

On a late summer evening in 1995, Susan Hurd, her brother and an assortment of friends gathered around a campfire at a fishing lodge. The conversation drifted somewhat and soon the group began exchanging spooky stories. Susan and her brother were able to contribute most convincingly for they had been raised in a haunted house. When one of the people who'd been listening to the siblings' first-hand account that night saw my request for Manitoba ghost stories, he contacted Susan who kindly responded with a nine-page letter documenting two, quite separate, family stories about hauntings.

The first story dates back to when she was just four years old. As is frequently the case with young children, Susan was apparently able to sense that which the older people were not.

"I should tell you that since [I was] a very young child I have believed wholeheartedly in life after death," Susan wrote candidly about her family's experiences with her uncle, a musician.

She went on to explain, "I have memories of my Uncle Wally laying on the sofa in his large and luxurious living room asking me to come to him."

The request terrified the usually friendly and extroverted child. "I can feel my stomach flip-flopping, the feeling of panic now as I ran past him to the front door only to find that I couldn't get out. I was four years old at the time and as I cannot remember ever being shy I contribute the fear to the fact that I knew he was going to die."

Apparently, despite his youth, Susan's Uncle Wally did die within the year.

"[M]y mother and Wally's wife had encounters with him prior to his burial. My grandparents purchased the large house with the music studios in the basement and my aunt and other music teachers continued to use the studios. I remember sitting in the room with the piano [Wally was a pianist] and talking to my uncle at length about how the family was and how much he was missed. I never saw him and never heard him but really felt his presence."

It is interesting that Susan felt fearful in her uncle's company while he was dying but not after his death. Her awareness of his returned spirit isn't at all unusual. Children often don't require the visual or auditory reinforcements that adults do to convince them of their paranormal experience. Wally's spirit was, however, seen by Susan's grandmother—always at his beloved piano.

An International Ghost Story

Over the years seances have come in and out of vogue as a form of entertainment. Contacting those who have "gone before" has, in different eras, been regarded by many as something of a parlour game. This interest in things paranormal likely came to Canada along with immigrants from Europe and the British Isles, for the practice had been popular there for years. People would routinely invite friends, neighbours and family members into their homes and at some point in the evening, those with such interests would gather around a table and attempt, either through a type of Ouija board, an actual medium or just using the table itself, to contact the spirits of the dead.

The following story illustrates this custom and its success. It seems that a group of approximately two dozen devotees had gathered at the home of an English family living in Goteburg, Sweden. No sooner had they begun their quest for spiritual contact than an apparition appeared before the entire, and no doubt amazed, group.

The ghost calmly explained to those seated around the table that although he had been a Swede by birth he had, two years before, emigrated to an area of Canada that would eventually be known as Manitoba. The phantom went on to explain that he had been unable to appear to his friends and relatives in the north of Sweden to let them know of his demise. As he knew his grieving widow in Canada would be too distressed to carry out the obligation, he had come this evening to ask the members of this group if one of them would be so kind as to pass along the sad news to those he had left behind in the Old Country.

While the folks at the amateur seance were attempting to understand what was going on in front of them, one of their members had the presence of mind to go in search of a camera. The ghost's image disappeared as quickly as it had appeared but fortunately not before his image was captured on film.

The shocked visitors and their hosts could hardly believe the success they'd had that night and the very next day set out to discover whether or not they'd been victims of a hoax. They sent a letter to a well-known Swede who had since settled in Canada. They asked him whether there had been a man fitting the description of their ghostly visitor who had recently died in the Assiniboia district.

Upon receiving the letter, the man immediately began making inquiries. Within days he was able to confirm that yes, such a man had been living nearby and had recently died. Further, his widow had, in fact, not yet made contact with those in Sweden who would have wanted to know.

Presumably, once all of the information the ghost had given the group had been confirmed, one or more of the Swedish seance-participants carried out the dead man's request and contacted his friends and family to advise them of his death.

On a final, rather frustrating note, this story was apparently originally released by the *Winnipeg Tribune* but picked up by other western Canadian papers, including the *Macleod Gazette* where I was directed to find it. The article ends with a comment about the photograph taken the evening of the highly successful seance: the photo was reported to be "a perfect likeness" and a "rather good" detailing of "the head and a portion of the shoulders." The only criticism offered about the picture indicated that it was "misty in appearance."

What a shame that those pioneer journalists were not able to reproduce the photograph in the newspaper where it could have been preserved for all time. The technology of the day, or lack thereof, dictated that we must be forever satisfied with a word picture.

Sarah and Her Descendants

Radio show host Bill Turner, of CKLQ in Brandon, has, over the years, developed something of a "following" for himself and his show. As a result, when he opens the phone lines for listeners to call he frequently recognizes their voices and knows something of their personalities.

When a caller with a distinct manner of speaking came on the line, Bill commented, "You sound nervous today, Mary."

For him, this was clearly somewhat of a surprise. He'd apparently spoken with the woman on the radio many other times but she had never revealed such a depth of emotion before. For me the evident tension I heard in her voice was no surprise. With almost one hundred percent consistency, people find re-telling a ghost story a highly emotional experience.

Mary hadn't been born and raised in Canada, another factor that was easy to determine by listening to her. Mary Murray is from England, a place where presumptions of ghosts and hauntings are far more accepted than they are here in Canada.

Perhaps this background helped to predispose the woman to accept the paranormal presence that had been a part of her family's life for a dozen years.

One of the topics that host Bill Turner and I discussed was how frequently museums are haunted. I shared my theory that as museums (and archives, too, for that matter) are caches of artifacts—each with its own history—they are frequently home to ghosts.

Mary had never heard that theory before but, in the letter she wrote to me later that same day, she indicated her experience would support my premise.

"It's funny that you mentioned that sometimes spirits move into museums. We bought [an] old United Church building and moved it here in 1972. [We] started up our museum at that time. This was [also] about the time 'Sarah' made herself known. We had never associated one with the other until today."

Mary and her husband might never have noted the coincidence of timing before but they had certainly noted the arrival of "Sarah" the ghost. The phantom's pranks began with the door of a cabinet that hung above their baby daughter Marie's crib. The ghost seemed to prefer the door open, while Mary had a preference for the cabinet door being closed.

"One day while [the baby] was sleeping, I closed it three times," the mother recalled.

She knew the door hadn't simply swung open of its own volition, as "it had a tight catch. The last time I shut it firmly and said, 'Now leave it closed' and it did."

When the Murrays' first daughter was two, the young parents welcomed the arrival of Melanie, their second daughter. The spirit with the penchant for opening cupboard doors soon made her presence known to the younger girl.

"She told me one day that this girl was watching T.V. with her."

Perhaps that particular viewing was uneventful but like many ghosts Sarah was extremely attracted to the family T.V. set, and liked to play with it.

"She would turn the T.V. on at odd times or you could be watching a show and she'd turn it off—and not just once."

I wondered how the family was sure the ghost was a female. Mary answered my unspoken query most effectively in her letter.

"We saw her many times going across the hall or from the porch to the living room. ..."

An apparition, that is the actual sighting of a ghost, is most unusual and certainly went a long way to explaining the family's conviction that the spectre was female but I was still curious about the use of the moniker "Sarah." This name had evidently not been an arbitrary choice. Mary explained, "One night I woke up suddenly, sat up in bed and woke my husband with a start and said, 'Her name's Sarah Pinguey.'"

Understandably, the woman's husband was puzzled. "He didn't know what the heck I was talking about."

Mary wasn't about to let that middle-of-the-night insight slip away. "It was really weird. I was going through the Murray records and came across the name in the family tree. Apparently, the vision's parents came out on a wagon train to Manitoba. On the way, their daughter, Sarah, died of some illness. Some of her family ended up here and possibly some of their things are in our museum."

At least now they had some sort of an explanation as to why their home became haunted, but they still had to decide what to do about it.

Predictably, the Murrays' children were the most likely members of the household to be aware of Sarah.

"Marie would not close her bedroom door because ... [Sarah] would be behind it. If [Marie] came home from school and was in the house alone, she could feel, rather than see [the ghost]. Marie would play the piano until I came home or Sarah went away."

The immediate family members were not the only ones to realize that there was something strange about the property the Murrays lived on.

"Our niece by marriage would not come into our house alone. On one occasion I was in the hospital and [our niece] came in here alone and was scared silly by Sarah." Unfortunately, Mary didn't include the details of that particular instance, but she did go on to explain that there were other occurrences.

"Whenever [our] niece came into our yard and we were not home the lights would go on and off. [The] other people with her verified this."

Although the Murrays' daughters had clearly developed the coping mechanisms they needed to share their lives with a ghost, the adults had had just about enough.

"As the years went on, Marie became more bothered by [Sarah]. This was when we mentioned [the haunting] to our minister ... He arranged for another minister and himself to come but didn't tell us when. He said 'they' would know and be prepared. One afternoon they came and we had this service in our living room. It was a weird feeling. We all held hands while they chanted. Our minister seemed to be affected the most."

People have many different ways to describe the sensation of knowing a ghost is around. A common description includes a reference to the change in a room's air pressure. Mary used a variation of that explanation to convey the change she felt in her home after the ministers had left.

"[T]he air seemed lighter," Mary told me before adding that her daughter Marie had noticed a difference immediately upon returning from school and had spontaneously used a very similar phrase: "The air's different."

Mary added, "She [Marie] played the piano just for the fun of it. It was lovely to see."

Since that time the Murray's children have grown into successful adults with lives of their own. Sarah has not returned. However, Mary still remembers and heeds the ministers' warning to take care not to invite her back, because they felt the spirit was growing in strength and had the potential to become a threat to the family's security.

Chapter 4

HAUNTED BY HISTORY

The Andree Ghosts Strike Again?

The following appeared in the St. Patrick's Day (March 17) issue of the *Winnipeg Free Press*—in the year 1898. Judging by the structure of the piece, you might be forgiven for thinking that paragraphs were not invented until the turn of the century. Of course, that is not so, but as you can see either the letter writer, editor or typesetter chose not to interrupt his story with even one paragraph break. We re-tell the story here in its ghostly entirety.

"GHOSTS IN THE NORTH," read the headline. It was followed by a subhead reading, "A Fisherman's Story of Midnight 'Spooks' Perfect Pandemonium Prevails in a Winnipegosis Fishing Camp—'Spirit' Will Not Speak."

Next, a journalist whose name has by now been lost, added the following sentence:

The following letter reached the *Free Press* by the Dauphin mail and is given space, as the writer thereof appears to be perfectly sincere in his statements that "spooks"—probably the Andree ghosts—are rambling about in the northern portions of our province:

To the Editor of the Free Press.

Sir, With your permission, I would like to give your readers a brief account of some strange phenomena existing at present in this fishing camp, near Red Deer Point, in this camp, about thirty-five miles from Winnipegosis station. The first time we noticed anything was on Wednesday, the 9th inst. There were five of us in the camp at the time, D.S. Nichols, of Mossy River, D.H. Mason, of Alliston, Ont., two Norwegians and myself. We were seated round the table shortly after 9 p.m., when we heard a loud, rasping noise at one of the windows, which was kept up almost continuously until nearly midnight. At intervals, also, we could hear what appeared to be something dragging along the roof, and a rattling and banging of the pipes. We could find nothing to account for these noises, though we did our best to do so. The next night, about the same time, we heard the ringing of a small bell, apparently near the stable. We were expecting our foreman back from the station, and thought nothing of this at first, although he had no bell on his horse when he left. We heard it again shortly after, and as no one appeared, we went out to see and though it was clear moonlight, we could discover nothing. The bell rang again; this time close to the camp. Then it rang inside the camp, and has done so every night more or less frequently, and is ringing to-night more than ever, having commenced about two hours earlier. The same noises went on as before, but more loudly. On Friday night tin dishes were thrown off the wall and the shelves with considerable force. Just after we had blown out our lamp about 11 p.m., it seemed as if all the boots and rubbers in the camp were being thrown about and the noise on the roof was very loud. Mr. A. Stewart, of Birtle, foreman for Mr. P. McArthur, of Westbourne, whose logging camp is near us, was with us on Friday night a part of the time, and on Saturday night several of his men came over to see for themselves, so that we had plenty of witnesses for the still more curious freaks of that night. Dishes were thrown all over the floor, a heavy iron stove, three or four feet out on the floor, and a dipper was not only thrown out of the pot, but replaced. A hat of one of McArthur's men, hanging on a nail about five feet from him, was put on his head, and shortly after thrown off. While I was writing, the paper was pulled out of my hand, and a large German

stocking was flung twice into the air, the last time hitting me on the head. However, to be brief, the climax was reached about 10:30 p.m. I had noticed for some time previously a slight oscillation of the table and a corresponding oscillation of the lamp. Suddenly the lamp went out, and then it was pandemonium let loose. Everything in the camp seemed to be on the move, the blows on the window were delivered with apparently sledgehammer force; the stoves rattled and shook, while the roof noise was very loud and there was also a loud knocking at the door. This happened three times, and then gradually the disturbances became less and ceased as usual shortly before midnight. It is now 10 p.m. [the next night] and things are again on the move, amongst others, two large pillows have been flung out on the floor. If any of your readers could furnish me with a satisfactory solution of these occurrences, I would be much obliged. I have several times asked the spirit, if it be a spirit, to speak, but receive no answer. In conclusion, I may say I am nearly twenty-one years in this country and am known to a good many, among others, Dr. E. Benson, who, I think, would vouch for my credibility.
A.C. O'Beirne, Winnipegosis, Man. March 13.

There is little doubt that the group camped near Red Deer Point was witness to some very dramatic poltergeist activity. The journalist's reference to an "Andree ghost" might mean little to today's readers but in 1898, when the story was written, an allusion to Dr. Salomon August Andree (1854–97), the Scandinavian balloonist, would have meant a great deal.

According to paranormal researcher W. Ritchie Benedict, Andree was something of a daredevil for his time and was blessed, according to Benedict, with "matinee-idol good looks." On July 11, 1897, he and three companions set off on an attempt to cross the North Pole in a balloon.

"He believed he was quite prepared for any contingency, including a crash," Benedict added.

Despite Andree's efforts to equip himself for a safe voyage, he and his crew effectively disappeared shortly after take-off. At first there were a few scattered reports of sightings in the far north of Norway but nothing more substantial—until 1930, when an encampment was found on White Island, not far from Spitsbergen, Norway.

According to Benedict, "As far as anyone could tell [Andree and his companions] had died of carbon monoxide poisoning from the kerosene stove. Ironically, had it not been for that, they conceivably could have survived and signalled a ship in the spring. There are actually photographs of the expedition's final days in existence. The photographic plates were perfectly preserved by the cold and were developed nearly a quarter of a century later. Some portions of the journal [the air ship's crew] kept, survived as well. Almost certainly they were all dead by late October, 1897. Their balloon trip had lasted all of three days."

This physical reality did not prevent world-wide reports of "phantom Andree" sightings. These were given great attention in the press and so would have made the reporter's reference at the beginning of this story immediately understandable and even somewhat comforting. There might be ghosts in the north of the province but at least they are familiar ones.

Clock Chimes Death

The number of ghost stories I've collected over the years has taught me that people will often keep a paranormal experience a secret for a good long time before sharing it with anyone. The following story, however, must nearly be a record for the longest kept secret. This story ran in the February 12, 1964, edition of *News of the North* and the incident occurred in July of 1918.

The person relating the story gave her name as Mrs. Chas McKenzie and indicated that, at the time of the telling, she lived in Roblin.

During the summer of 1918, however, she apparently lived near Dauphin on a farm with her parents. On that particular day in July, she and her mother were the only ones home. Her mother was in the bedroom and the future Mrs. McKenzie was in the bathroom, which she explained was just off the kitchen.

Mrs. McKenzie went on to describe the kitchen clock as being one that her parents had brought with them in 1907 when they made the trek from Ontario to Manitoba. The clock had a pendulum mechanism that was in full working order when the adventurous young couple left their home in the east.

"For some reason this clock had refused to run in its new home and had stood silently on the shelf for more than 11 years," Mrs. McKenzie attested.

The clock was the farthest thing from either of women's minds at the time, for they were both very concerned about a little neighbour, a three-year-old boy named Clifford. He had, just the day before, been taken to the hospital suffering from "brain fever."

"Suddenly on this July afternoon, though absolutely untouched and undisturbed, the old clock struck, boldly and clearly, three times."

Mrs. McKenzie's mother sadly accepted that the chiming clock was a message from the beyond. "That must mean that Clifford is dead or dying," she surmised.

By bedtime that night Mrs. McKenzie and her mother had received word that indeed the three year old had died just as their broken clock unexpectedly chimed three times. As soon as they heard the news, the women knew the sounds from the usually silent clock were Clifford's way of saying good-bye to them.

Phantom at Fairford

Researcher W. Ritchie Benedict's specialty is apparently obscure references, for who else would have thought to look in the Champion, Alberta, *Chronicle* (dateline October 21, 1920) for a Fairford, Manitoba, ghost story?

This historical ghost story was told by a Hudson's Bay Company employee, calling himself by the Cree name "O-GE-MAS-ES," which he considerately translated as "Little Clerk." Presumably the following was the man's second paranormal experience. The first can be found in this book's story on ghost lights (see p. 219).

Little Clerk indicates the following eerie events took place the same year as when he had been followed halfway across Lake Manitoba by a ghost light. If we can extrapolate from the information he gave surrounding his previous story, it is safe to assume the events took place sometime in the 1870s. Despite the passage of approximately 125 years, this ghost story is still very unnerving.

Little Clerk was ordered by Chief Factor Archie McDonald to take charge of the Fairford post. The place had apparently stood abandoned for some time and now there was a considerable amount of preparation necessary before it could become a manned, viable operation once again. McDonald's instructions to Little Clerk were clear and direct. Upon reaching Fairford, he was to set immediately to work constructing a main residence. From there he was to clear all the existing buildings of any useful articles and then set fire to them all.

Although the fort was, at that time, old enough to have seen much better days, this measure still seemed extreme and somewhat wasteful. As discreetly as possible, Little Clerk inquired as to why the Chief Factor would issue such an order. Perhaps anticipating that the man would have questions, McDonald was ready to justify his reasons.

"Oh, there are some fool stories current at Fairford as to the [buildings] being haunted, for some bloody rows took place there in the old drinking days."

Such an explanation, of course, merely provoked more questions than it answered. When Little Clerk arrived at Fairford, he organized an extra-large work party to construct the new main residence and then began to ask questions about the story his boss had only hinted at. Specifically, he was curious as to "what shape [if any] the spooks were supposed to take?"

Typically, those people he asked were hesitant to commit to any specific goings-on but he was, at least, able to determine that the native peoples living in this area refused to stay near the post after dark. As Little Clerk thought of himself as the most rational of men, he dismissed the little he had heard as nonsense. That night he and his cook, a man named Malcolm, stayed alone in the abandoned fort. Well, not quite alone for Little Clerk was rarely without his canine companions, "my four famous dogs Herod, Nero, Moro and Hero." As long as they were with him (and apparently they always were), he felt secure. "If anyone touched me, [they] would have had a bad time of it as they [the dogs] were exceedingly fierce if set on any person or animal."

Little Clerk described the layout of the fort as being a quadrangle surrounded by a boardwalk. Like the buildings, the walk had apparently become dilapidated until, by the time of this telling, it was actually difficult to walk around the fort on the boardwalk without having a number of boards lift up and then bang back down.

As Little Clerk settled in for the night, he was surprised to see his cook approaching him. Malcolm seemed to have a rather embarrassed look about him. He was coming to inform his superior that he would not be spending the night in the old fort. Malcolm explained that he knew he would be unable to sleep for "he kept hearing noises ... and also felt things moving though he could see nothing."

Little Clerk felt he had no alternative but to let the man have his way, and after Malcolm had left he searched the place thoroughly for clues as to what had actually frightened the man. He found nothing out of the ordinary, but nonetheless got out an old shotgun and called his dogs to him. He opened the window in the room where he'd intended to sleep but pulled the blind down. This way, he figured, he could hear anyone if they should approach and yet the blind would keep out unwanted light and insects.

By the time he had executed all these precautions, it was nearly midnight and Little Clerk reported he was more than ready for a night's sleep.

"Just as I was falling asleep I heard a heavy trampling noise coming round the square on the platforms. I was out of bed like a flash, cocked my gun and waited developments. The heavy tramping came right on past my window but there was nothing visible, though the night was light enough to see the other buildings plainly. As the noise passed the window, I thought I could detect a draught of cold air," he explained before admitting, "It is no use disguising the fact that I felt creepy."

Moments later, the tramping sounds stopped. Little Clerk could do nothing except wait. His patience was rewarded and within minutes the heavy footfalls of the invisible intruder started up again. He could trace the phantom thuds as they progressed along the boardwalk from the main fort entrance to "past the ... store, then turning in front of my window."

Terrified of the unseen force, Little Clerk "threw the front door open and set the dogs on it. Out they went with furious growls and back they came again, hair bristling up and evidently cowed, as they retreated into the corner." They would "make no response" when their master "urged them out again."

If the dogs were not brave enough to face whatever was out there, Little Clerk was certainly loath to and yet what alternative did he have? The fort, its men and their safety were all his responsibility.

"I could see nothing but this time distinctly felt a cold draught [of] air pass. The dogs either felt or saw something that scared them, [but they] may be ... more sensitive to non-visible auras or whatever name it or they might be called than the human kind—or has civilization dulled our perceptive faculties?"

Although he never gave up trying, Little Clerk never did see the noisy presence that haunted the Fairford post. Bravely, however, he did stay on task.

"I became used to the racket. It was several weeks before the new residence was ready for occupancy and during this time I constantly heard the same heavy tramplings and other noises and there was no doubt the dogs were affected, as generally they were joyous creatures always ready to sport or play with me. I was glad enough, after vacating the premises, to put a torch to the old fort."

Much to the disappointment of today's ghost story lovers, neither researcher W. Ritchie Benedict nor I were ever able to find a trace of Little Clerk anywhere else in any of the archival newspapers we checked. What a shame! It would have been most satisfying to have had some closure on this eerie old story. As it is, we are left with no idea as to whether the spirit left the area of the fort once his old "haunts" had been destroyed by fire. It is, of course, equally possible that he stayed, unnerving hundreds of Fairford residents for further decades, but Little Clerk's services were needed elsewhere so he was not there to record the facts. We are left to wonder not only who the ghost could have been but also when and where he went.

Ham's Haunted House

I've often heard people explain that one building or another is haunted because it stands on land that was once a native people's burial ground. This is the explanation offered for this story, which is included in journalist George H. Ham's autobiographical work, *Reminiscences of a Raconteur*. The book was published in 1921, but the events that follow apparently took place almost forty-five years before the book's release. At that time George Ham and his wife lived in a haunted house, which they rented from a gentleman by the name of Captain George Young.

In 1877 when the ghostly events took place, the house was located on Main Street in Winnipeg, "just south of the old Grace Church."

Thanks to Ham's autobiography, we can read the story today as George Ham himself told it.

"During the night queer noises were heard. The stove in the adjoining room rattled like mad, and investigation proved nothing. There was no wind or anything else visible that should cause a commotion. A door would slam and on going to it, it was found wide open. One night there was a loud noise as if some tinware hanging up on the wall in the kitchen had fallen ... and so it went on," Ham began.

"One time the cellar was filled with water coming from where, goodness only knows, though it was said that there was a slough through that property years ago. Anyway, the cellar was full of water, and it had to be bailed out," he reported.

To clean the water up quickly, Ham's wife hired some local boys. "But lo and behold, when the trap door [to the cellar] was opened, there wasn't a drop of water in the blooming cellar. It was dry as a tin horn. We never ascertained whence came the water or where it went, but by this time I had got accustomed to the prances and pranks of the house and didn't care. ..."

The strange occurrences continued until the Hams moved out in 1880. Ham reflected on his period of residency: "I don't pretend to be able to explain the queer noises. Whether they were the spirits of the past and gone, Indian braves showing their displeasure at our intrusion in their domain, or were caused by some peculiarity in the construction of the house and its environments, I can not [sic] offer an opinion. But as we got accustomed to them, they didn't disturb us at all, and we got rather proud of our ghostly guests whose board and lodging cost us nothing."

The next tenant to occupy the haunted house was a tobacco merchant named Conlisk. The poltergeist activity continued during his stay in the place, but unlike the Hams, he was decidedly uncomfortable with his paranormal roommate and so he cut his residency short, staying only a month.

By 1881 Captain Young was apparently discouraged with the business of being a landlord and sold the property to a man named McVicar. At that point the house was moved to a location in what was then considered the north side of Winnipeg. When Ham happened by the new location and recognized his former haunted house, he immediately knocked on the door. He was curious as to whether the noises had continued even after the building had been moved. Understandably, the current occupants wouldn't let the man in. The building was eventually demolished in 1910 and so we will never know whether or not the spirits travelled with it. It has been recorded, however, that the move had not gone smoothly.

None of this, however, interfered with McVicar's plans. He built the McVicar Block on the previously residential lot and the building remained there for many years. Rumours of ghostly activity hovered in and around the "new" building for the forty years that it stood. It wasn't until 1922 when the stately old building was demolished that a possible clue to the haunting in the previous century finally surfaced.

Excavation unearthed four skeletons—probably belonging to long-deceased members of a nearby native tribe. When archaeologists were called in to investigate further, it was determined that the lot on which (first) the house and then the McVicar Block had stood had earlier been a native burial ground and was, in fact, rich with artifacts. It is a location that all Winnipeggers know well, for it is very near The Forks.

The Ghost of Henry Hudson

The oldest Canadian ghost story I have been able to find, west of the Maritimes, was reported in the February 21, 1878, edition of *The Daily Free Press*. By Canadian standards that date is a very long way back in history. What makes this report even more amazing, however, is that the event it records occurred two centuries prior to the article being published.

The story was reported to the *Free Press* from York Factory on the shores of Hudson Bay. Apparently, an employee of the

Hudson's Bay Company was "searching among the archives of this old ... post [and] came upon a singular collection of relics."

The newspaper account continues, "... perhaps the most interesting discovery [in the archival collection] is that of a ... French manuscript, written in 1618 by one who signs himself, 'Louis Marin, mariner.'"

Poor Louis, it would seem, had sailed with Henry Hudson on the failed leader's third and final attempt to find the Northwest Passage. History tells us that the explorers' ship, the *Discovery*, was as inadequate for the job at hand as Henry Hudson was as a leader. The adventurers had left England in 1610. By June of that year, Hudson and his company had reached the shores of the bay now named for Henry. The beleaguered party spent a dreadful winter on shore and by the following spring were a dejected, disheartened lot, wanting only to sail for home.

When the ice in the bay began to break-up, Hudson announced that he had no intention of returning to England without first finding the elusive passage to the riches of the Orient. No longer able to believe in its leader's ability to make wise judgements, the crew mutinied. Hudson, his son and a number of crew members, who had gone blind over winter, were set adrift in a small craft to face certain and imminent death.

The mutineers then headed back to England in the *Discovery.* Marin wrote, "[W]e headed the ship out that night and in the morning the pinnace [the boat in which the disposed leader, his son and the disabled sailors were stranded] had disappeared. I became afraid of the crew and of the ship for every night at midnight the ghosts of the captain and the ... blind sailors came aboard and troubled us sorely."

Poor Marin and his crewmates. They had survived the voyage across the Atlantic in the pathetically inadequate *Discovery*, and lived through a winter in which many of the sailors lost their sight as a result of poor diet, only to be frightened nearly half to death by ghosts.

A postscript to this ghostly piece of our early history—four of the nine surviving mutineers were tried for murder but were absolved of their guilt. That ruling probably more accurately reflected the value to the English economy of the sailors' knowledge of the Northwest Passage than it did the court's opinion of the mutineers' guilt.

If the ghosts of Hudson and his men still roam the frozen shores near York Factory, they no doubt do so in peace by now, for that community, the earliest permanent settlement in Manitoba, is now a ghost town. The post is being preserved as a National Historic Site, but the area's harsh climate is taking its toll. The few remaining buildings, and even the land on which those buildings sit, are steadily crumbling. Soon the area will, once again, be as barren as it was when the crew from the *Discovery* sentenced its leader to death.

Real-Estate Wraith

Over the years people have tried in a number of disparate ways to either prove or disprove the existence of ghosts. Some of those attempts at establishing proof have been scientific, others quasi-scientific, while still others, such as seances and Ouija board sessions, depend on the further mechanics of spiritualism. Occasionally, even our legal system has been called upon to become involved with determining whether the dead ever come back to haunt us.

In many ways, this latter situation seems a pairing of two

totally dissimilar elements of our culture. The law is, by nature and necessity, pragmatic and impassive. It strength lies in hard evidence. The world of the paranormal, however, is more like a religion in that it is based on faith and supposition. The law and the paranormal must, therefore, be considered to be at opposite ends of a continuum. Despite this, however, the two have occasionally been called together to form a sort of conceptual odd couple. Such was the case in Winnipeg in the first decade of the twentieth century.

It all began the week before Halloween in 1905 when the *Manitoba Free Press* ran an article, not once but three times in three separate issues, stating that the "second house east of Main Street on St. John's Avenue is believed by some people to be haunted at night between 11 and 12 midnight."

The piece then went on to describe "parties of men hanging around the house ... awaiting the appearance of the spook," before adding that the "house is, at present, unoccupied."

The description of the suspected entity is a woefully inadequate one for ghost-lovers. "There is a ghost in the north end of the city that is causing a lot of trouble to the inhabitants [of the area]. His chief haunt is in a vacant house on St. John's Avenue near to Main. He appears late at night and performs strange antics so that timid people give the place a wide berth."

Although it's disappointing that the pioneer reporter left his readers wondering what "trouble" was caused or what "strange antics" were performed by the wraith, he apparently couldn't resist giving the story a bit of a spin through the use of humour.

"A number of men have lately made a stand against ghosts in general and at night they rendezvous in the basement and close around the haunted house to await his ghostship but so far he remains at large."

The *Winnipeg Telegram* apparently ran a similar article that week and the combination of the news stories served to authenticate the ghostly rumours that had been floating around the north-end community for some weeks. Following these newspaper reports, unruly crowds gathered in the area and the unoccupied house, which was accepted as the vortex of the haunting, was damaged.

For a couple of early-day Winnipeggers, the timing could not have been worse. One of the two was a physician named Dr. Kelly. He had just arranged to buy the house with an eye to converting it to a private hospital. He had secured his offer to purchase with a $250 deposit and a commitment to tender a further $4,750 on October 24, 1905, coincidentally, the day after the first article about the house being haunted appeared.

When the good doctor read the write-up about his recently negotiated real-estate investment, Kelly was aghast. He refused to follow through on the contract and in so doing, forfeited the money he'd given to secure the transaction.

The vendor, a woman named Mrs. Nagy, was the other citizen in Manitoba's capital who was disturbed by the newspaper reports. She was, understandably, angry. She'd thought she'd sold her large and long-empty house. Now it looked as though the deal had needlessly fallen through because a local scribe had an idea for a pre-Halloween story. Nagy sued the *Free Press* newspaper which, rather interestingly, defended itself by protesting that it knew the ghost story was not true and that it had been allowed to run as a joke.

This disclaimer, of course, did nothing to calm Mrs. Nagy who maintained that she had suffered a financial loss as a result of what the newspaper was now brushing off as nothing more than a prank. At the ensuing trial Dr. Kelly's evidence did not help Nagy's case. His testimony gave the presiding judge, Justice Macdonald, reason to believe that the physician was actually only using the publication of the "haunted house" story as a ruse to back out of a deal that no longer suited his needs. You see, while on the witness stand, the doctor let information slip that he wished to avail himself of a recently presented opportunity to move to Vancouver.

But the case was far from settled at that point. Next, a lawyer for the plaintiff, a learned Mr. Leech, trotted out the Bible as evidence and there pointed to passages in both Genesis and Job where it is explained "that Abraham, Isaac and Job all 'gave up the ghost.'" This reference was questioned on the grounds that there was no record of any of them ever having come back. The tenacious Leech, obviously knew his Bible for he chose yet another passage: "[T]he Mount of Transfiguration ... the spirits of the departed [were] there and [were] recognized." That quotation, he protested, "proved there were ghosts and spirits."

When it became evident that his Biblical references were not completely convincing to all, the ingenious lawyer turned to linguistics. He read aloud the dictionary definition for the word "ghost" and added that every nationality's language reflected such a concept. Therefore, he reasoned, "the *Free Press* had published a story which they knew would reach many persons whom they knew would be influenced by the report. The proof of direct loss was that a purchaser had refused to take the house after the report had been published."

Despite all of Leech's clever legal wranglings, the judge ruled that the value of Mrs. Nagy's house had not been lowered by the ghost story's publication.

But that did not settle the matter. By April of 1907, the case was before an Appeals Court. In the end Mrs. Nagy was awarded $1,000 and presumably everyone was then, reasonably content. In addition to that money, Nagy had the doctor's initial deposit and, of course, she still had her house in the north end of the city. The lawyers had their fees and Dr. Kelly could make his move to Lotus Land unencumbered by any unwanted real-estate investment.

Yes, almost everyone was happy. Of course, those of us who love a ghost story are left with dozens and dozens of unanswered questions. Our frustrations, though, are no doubt slight compared to those the ghost himself must have felt. Imagine the humiliation of having your entire existence written off as a joke.

An Old Family Story

The following ghost story has been passed down through Manitoba's Cockerill family, and Cheryl Cockerill Arlein, of Leaf Rapids, was kind enough to forward it to me.

The incident began either in the fall of 1908 or the winter of 1909 and considerably south of Cheryl's present home. It seems that at that time her ancestor, William Cockerill, opened a saw mill at "Crerar Lake, known locally as Dark Lake," she began.

"One evening in about 1908, a man came to the farm and was asking directions [about] how to get to the bush. Presumably he was asking how to get to the forest reserve to hide. He said he was in trouble with the police in Grandview ... that they were looking for him."

The wanted man had rather an odd appearance. "He had a pair of pants hung around his neck by the suspenders and the legs [of those pants] were stuffed full of something. Over his shoulder he carried a stick and on the end of the stick was tied a red hanky that was also stuffed with something."

He warned Cockerill that the police would undoubtedly be on his trail. No one ever saw the man again nor did the police ever make any inquiries.

"When the mill opened at Dark Lake a mysterious thing … happened," Cheryl's letter continued. "They heard knocking. The knocking was not confined to any one particular place—it was heard on the ceiling, walls, floor and even in the middle of a frozen rain barrel. They came to the conclusion that the [unexplained] knocking was a ghost, possibly the man who had visited their farm earlier on."

The mill operators were receptive to the idea that they had a spirit in their presence, after the spirit made these initial rudimentary communications.

"As time went on they started to communicate with the ghost. It was mainly done by knocking. They would ask the ghost questions and it would answer by knocking three times for 'yes' and two times for 'no.'"

Little changed once that pattern had been established until the escaped man's ghost took exception to a woman who occasionally had reason to be at the mill.

"Patty Woodhouse [was] an unbeliever," Cheryl stated. "[This] roused the ghost's anger. It would pull at her hair and sometimes it would even pull some right out. The falling hair would make weird patterns wherever it fell. [The ghost] would also scratch her arms until it drew blood."

About that time, for reasons that have become lost through the years, Patty and her sister Annette decided to have their pictures taken. "Each took turns sitting on the same chair to have their picture taken. Annette's picture turned out very clear, while Patty's picture was just a blurry shadow but the chair was clearly visible through the shadow." Both women credited the ghost, and his hostile feelings for Patty, with causing the odd photographic results.

Another time when people were visiting the mill, they no sooner mentioned the ghost than phantom knocking started up "to let them know he was there."

Despite the spirit's occasional hostility to outsiders, Cheryl reported, "The family was never afraid of the ghost because at no time did it try to harm any of them. It was said that if you believed that the ghost existed it would never harm you, but people who did not believe that it was there roused its anger."

On another occasion a man named "Billy Angus stopped at Dark Lake mill on his way to Bield one evening. They persuaded him to stop overnight, rest his horses and have something to eat. During the course of the conversation after supper, they told him about the ghost that was at the mill."

That was all the recognition the phantom needed to begin his hijinks. For, "shortly afterwards a quilt started to move about on the bed like a mink or something was under it trying to get out. When they lifted the quilt, there was nothing there. Everyone went to bed shortly thereafter and they don't know if the ghost bothered Billy or if he was just uneasy about it but by two in the morning Billy was already up and gone."

An especially unnerving event took place through the night. "Everyone slept in feather beds," Cheryl began. "One night a lump raised up in the middle of the bed. William [Cockerill] grabbed a knife. He cut the mattress open but there was nothing there."

One time the ghost really showed off the strength of his energy. "A calendar was knocked off the wall. William happened to mention the fact that the calendar was on the floor and all at once the calendar started up the wall in a snake-like fashion. On getting up as far as the nail, it couldn't manage to hook itself back onto the nail so it fell to the floor again."

At first, communication between the living and spectral occupants of the mill was restricted to communication by tappings and the odd ghostly trick. This limited communication was somewhat frustrating to the Cockerills. "It seemed like the ghost was always trying to tell them something but they could never figure it out." Eventually, "they changed from knocking for 'yes' and 'no' to tapping out the alphabet."

Using a planchette similar to the kind associated with Ouija boards, Annette Cockerill and her mother Ada were finally able to "talk" to their resident presence.

"The ghost spelled out to them that he had been killed by a bear over by a certain tree near the mill. Ada went in search of this particular tree and in some windfall near the tree she found the bones of a human foot and leg. Also, on instruction from the ghost they went to dig for some money that was supposed to be buried there. No money was found at that time, only several pieces of cloth ... buried six to eight inches below the surface of the ground. They were tattered and torn quite badly and appeared to be quite old. Sometime later, [a male relative] did find some coins and part of an old shirt.

"After Ada found the foot and leg, she placed them into a bag and set the bag outside the cookshack door. When she returned for it, the bag was gone. After the bag disappeared, so did the ghost. He seemed satisfied and was never heard from again."

In an interesting postscript to this ghost story, descendants of the original mill owners visited Dark Lake in the summer of 1974. "They found an old coin there that dated back to the 1800s."

Because no one ever found out what the man was wanted for, or what he had stuffed in either his bandanna or the legs of the spare pants he had hung around his neck, it's as good a bet as any that the strange events are explained by the following: it was his spirit returning from the dead to let the family who had helped him know where they could find the money that was no longer of any use to him.

Cheryl (Cockerill) Arlein advised me that, in keeping with the ancestors' long tradition, she has, by now, passed the family ghost story on to her children.

Minister Receives Strange Message

It was a beautiful spring day in approximately the middle of April, 1912. The evening service at Winnipeg's Rosedale Methodist Church would begin in a few hours. Charles Morgan, the young minister, was a conscientious man who was in the habit of arriving at the church early on Sunday mornings and staying throughout the entire day. This day had been no exception and by evening he had everything ready for the final service of worship. He had even posted the numbers of the hymns to be sung on the notice board. With that final duty taken care of, all his obligations had been attended to and he sat down to rest.

In an attempt to refresh himself for the upcoming service, Morgan slipped into meditation. While in the trance-like state, a number flashed into his consciousness, not just once but twice. It seemed to the reverend to be a number of a hymn but certainly not one with which he was familiar.

Moments later, refreshed and invigorated, Charles Morgan set about greeting parishioners as they came into the church to worship. The service went smoothly, with the congregation singing the hymns he'd listed earlier in the day. Oddly, though, throughout the service the man could not shake the feeling that the numbers he'd seen while meditating were of a hymn and that for some reason it was important that the congregation sing that particular hymn before they left the church that evening.

In a drastic break with tradition, the young Reverend Charles Morgan called out the number that had been on his mind and accordingly, those attending the service sang it with him. Their rendition of the musical prayer completely lacked polish, however, because it was not a hymn any in the crowd were familiar with. After all, "Hear Father while we pray to Thee for those in peril on the sea" would not have been a standard choice for a church in a prairie city.

The congregation must have left the church that evening as puzzled as the minister himself was over his sudden diversion from the norm. Because the communications of that era were painfully slow and news often took many days to travel even halfway across the country, many of the congregation who had attended that late-day service at the Rosedale Methodist Church in Winnipeg on April 14, 1912 did not yet know about an historic event. As their dedicated young minister was calling out for them to sing an usual choice of hymn, the "unsinkable" *Titanic* was lurching at a precarious angle and about to disappear into the ice cold waters of the North Atlantic, taking hundreds of lives with her. One thousand five hundred and twenty-two lives to be precise, a number that might have been increased if Winnipeg businessman Mark Fortune and his son had not seen that Mrs. Fortune and her daughters were safely on board a lifeboat. After this duty, the two men returned to the *Titanic's* deck to join the other people who were singing and waiting for their inevitable deaths (see story, p. 55).

The Other Story of the Headless Statue

Not many people ask if the place they've just been hired to work in is haunted. Ten years ago, however, Janelle Reynolds did exactly that. What's more, no one was surprised by her question. You see Janelle's situation is a little unusual. She not only works at Riel House, but is a member of the executed leader's family.

"My grandmother slept upstairs here," she explained to me.

Riel House was built in 1880 as the family's home. Because of the tumultuous political events that occurred in that period, Louis Riel himself never actually lived in the house. It was, however, where his family lived when he was executed and therefore where the government shipped his body after the hanging. The courts may have judged him to be a traitor, but to the Metis, Riel was a hero and so, for a period of days, his body was laid out in Riel House while mourners came through to pay their respects.

Because Janelle Reynolds knew the details of the emotionally charged history surrounding the house, she had asked if it was haunted.

"One guide told me that she'd once felt a hand on her shoulder. I said, 'That must have been frightening.' But she said no, that it had given her a warm feeling," Janelle explained.

Today, after having worked at Riel House for ten years, listening to that allusion of a presence in the house is as close as Janelle Reynolds has come to experiencing a ghost in the historic building. Psychically speaking, at least, the house is surprisingly quiet.

"I do have one little anecdote that you might like," the soft-spoken history buff added.

Intrigued, I asked Janelle to tell it to me.

It seems there is a headless statue on a shelf in the living room at Riel House. "Ours is only a replica. The original is kept at the St. Boniface Museum. It's a statue of St. Joseph who is the patron saint of the Metis."

Legend has it that Riel was holding the statue when he was hanged. When the rope snapped, he dropped the statue, its head fell off and was lost in the crowd. When the government shipped Riel's body back to Manitoba, they included the headless statue as part of the man's personal effects. This story is the commonly accepted legend surrounding the strange artifact.

"Family history tells a different story," Janelle continued.

Riel's family could not get to Regina to be with him in his final hour so they did the only thing they felt they could to support him. "They assembled in Riel House and prayed."

Naturally, the statue of St. Joseph was a focal point for their prayers. Throughout the day, Riel's mother clutched the figure.

"At the exact time Riel was hanged, the head popped off the statue."

What eerie irony that both Riel's and the statue's necks broke at the same instant. Was this Riel's way of saying his final good-byes to his family, the only way he could, or was St. Joseph reacting to what he must have deemed a great injustice? Today, those questions are unanswerable, as is why one of the most fascinating potential haunts in the entire province of Manitoba remains nearly ghost-free.

Chapter 5

MANITOBA MEDLEY

Spirit Snippets

Because so many Manitoba ghost stories are old enough to have become folklore, the tales by now often have a ragged quality to them. They are not the neatly constructed stories that fictional ghost stories are. Authentic reports, unlike those contrived texts, will not, necessarily have specific beginnings or middles or even endings. They are often only fragments of a story. When this is so, the details that are missing can be as intriguing to ponder as those that are known.

The following reports are really a collection of some of these fragments. Anyone looking for completeness will come away disappointed, for, as with all the ghost stories in this book, these stories are not fictional accounts and I have refused to embellish any story just to conform to anyone's predetermined standards.

By coincidence, all the following stories took place either in or around Winnipeg.

The existence of ghosts is sometimes explained as being "leftover energy"—the residue of what once was that person's essence. That particular theory certainly helps to explain why ghosts are so attracted to sources of electrical activity. A house in the Elmwood area, not far from the old and once well-haunted Hamilton place (see p. 69), is home to a ghost with an attraction to electric light switches. The lights in the place turn on and off seemingly of their own accord when no one (visible) is near them. The ghost is thought to be a man who once lived in the house. After he has the lighting adjusted to suit his needs, he sits in an old rocking chair, contentedly rocking back and forth. Presumably, the motion is soothing to the ghost, but for the person watching an apparently empty chair rock back and forth it can understandably be a little stressful.

Have you ever noticed how some houses in a neighbourhood never seem to stay occupied while others are home to the same family for dozens and dozens of years? Of course, there are all kinds of reasons why a place could have a high turnover rate—it could have an inhospitable layout, awkward mortgaging arrangements or possibly even a ghost.

A house on Landsdowne Avenue meets the above description nicely. Over the years tenants have come and gone but no one has ever lived in the place for any length of time. A couple named Warren and Lorna Wilcox were among the tenants in the place and judging from what they say, it sounds as though the place has been home to a ghost for some time.

Doors will be heard opening and closing when there is no one, who can be seen, near them. The water faucets, another favourite plaything of ghosts, will turn on and off of their own volition. But most distressing of all is the haunting sound of a baby crying—when no baby can be found. Sadly, rumour has it that, many years ago, a baby was murdered in the house. The child's little soul has apparently been filling the atmosphere in the house with the injustice it must be suffering.

A house near the Disraeli Freeway is apparently so haunted that even the homeless won't seek shelter there on the worst nights of winter. No details of the haunting are available but a description of the place includes references to turrets—a feature that would definitely be attractive to a ghost looking for a residence.

There are two stories of haunted houses on Cathedral Avenue. Although they are both most assuredly ghost stories, they have evolved over years of telling and re-telling so that by now they also fall into the category of urban legend. These tales might actually be two versions of the same story.

An unfinished house on Cathedral Avenue is rumoured to have a most unpleasant history and is now very haunted. Few details remain, but the gist of the story indicates that a man hanged himself in the house. When his body was discovered, a couple of decidedly strange circumstances were noted. The stool on which the deceased must have stood to loop the noose around his neck was nowhere near the man's corpse. Where it was found positively defies explanation. The small stool was standing in a far-off corner—not lying on its side as though it had been kicked away, but standing upright as though it had purposefully been placed there.

The legend goes on to recount that, in response to some sort of a dare or a rite of passage, three teenaged boys stationed themselves in the house on Halloween night. They were apparently so traumatized by the experience that they have been hospitalized ever since.

Another Cathedral Avenue haunted house, also described as being abandoned, is a boarded-up duplex. For years high school students at Garden City Collegiate were convinced that there was a presence in the house. They spoke of a murder that had taken place there long ago, which had left the house with a decidedly uncomfortable atmosphere. By now there is no one who can substantiate those claims but, conversely, neither is there anyone to deny them.

Point Douglas, one of the oldest areas in Winnipeg, has had a long and colourful history. It would be surprising if at least a few buildings there were not haunted. The rumours that once circulated about "strange visitors" in a particular old Point Douglas house have not been heard recently. Perhaps the spirit's energy has faded by now or perhaps the ghost has merely moved on to more modern accommodations.

The McIntyre Building has long since met its fate in the form of a wrecker's ball. During its lifetime, however, it was said to be home to an apparition. Because the spirit revealed a preference to preserve the old place, it could be interesting to spend a night in its replacement.

Ghosts and bureaucrats are an admittedly unusual pairing, but the two found themselves entangled in the following ghost story. More than twenty-five years ago, a family had the sad task of burying a relative. The woman had been a widow for a number of years. Immediately following the funeral, and for several nights running, the apparition of the newly deceased woman made herself visible to five family members. She was most unhappy about the location chosen for her grave. It seems that she and her husband, who had been estranged for a number of years in life, were not able to lie peacefully in the side-by-side graves they had once purchased.

The relatives, therefore, had a real problem on their hands. They could hardly take it upon themselves to dig up the coffin and re-bury it in another location and yet neither could they endure the nightly visits from the woman's ghost. They decided to take the dilemma to the authorities. As can well be imagined, great debate followed. Eventually, the family was granted official permission to move the woman's casket to another location. Desperate for peace and quiet, they made the necessary arrangements right away and reported that the change of venue must have calmed the spirit's angst, for they have not seen her since.

Some years ago a man was seen standing, staring out of the window of his house, which was situated near the Luxton playground in Winnipeg's north end. Nothing unusual about that, of course—except that the day that sighting occurred, the man had been dead for some months.

Parks Canada historian Bob Coutts remembered there being a ghost story connected with an area along the old River Road. The community's milkman was going about his early morning rounds when suddenly he was startled to see a woman hurrying from the road towards the river. As he'd been covering the same route for years, he was well used to the area and the routines of the residents. For that reason, he knew it would be most unusual for anyone to even be out at that hour, let alone walking in a rush towards the river.

Thinking that the woman might need assistance, he stopped to ask what the problem might be and whether he could help. This closer examination only confused him further, for he saw that the woman rushing to the river bank was dressed in nineteenth-century attire. Worse, the image of the strange woman faded and then disappeared as he watched.

The milkman tried to put the image he'd seen that morning out of his mind, but he was not entirely successful. Eventually, he was so disturbed by what he'd seen that he began telling people about the sighting, describing where he'd seen the woman and what she looked like. Before long the man was forced to acknowledge that what many of these people were telling him was true. He'd seen a ghost.

Local history has it that in the previous century, a child drowned just at the spot where the milkman had seen the apparition. The drowning had been a terrible blow to his mother, of course, but especially because she'd been right there with him on the river bank and when she'd seen her boy was in trouble had immediately raced to his side. She'd been too late. The boy had drowned in just those few seconds. The mother had never forgiven herself for not having gotten to the lad in time and seemed doomed to repeat the failed dash into a heartbreaking eternity.

Haunted House for Sale

In 1991 a real-estate agent listed a large, old house in south Winnipeg for sale. The asking price was lower than comparable properties in the area and so the agent was puzzled that the "For Sale" sign on the lawn drew little interest. She began to talk to the owners of neighbouring houses to see if they could offer any insight. The agent soon had her answer, although it no doubt displeased her.

Neighbourhood scuttlebutt was that around the turn of the twentieth century a witch and her mentally handicapped son had owned the place. After the woman died and her son found other accommodation, the house was rented out to a long line of very transient tenants. When these people moved out, they did so quickly, never stopping to explain their sudden departure to the other residents of the block.

This pattern remained constant for years until a particular tenant moved into the suite on the top floor of the house. Like all of the previous owners, this man only stayed in the place a matter of weeks but, unlike those tenants who had gone before him, he took the time to explain to the neighbours that his leave-taking had nothing to do with the community. The man had apparently been aware since he first moved in that he was sharing his living space with a spirit. Although he'd never seen the ghost, he was sure there was one for, despite leaving the apartment neat each day, he would return to find it in disarray—toiletries and dishes strewn all about.

One day to test his theory about the place being haunted, the man left a tape recorder running in his empty apartment while he was out. It was listening to what was recorded on that tape that finally drove the man to seek alternate housing. He told the neighbours that it would be a long time before he would be able to forget the loud, unidentifiable noises and blood-curdling screams that he heard when he played the tape back.

This chilling anecdote explained a lot to the real-estate agent. Now she understood why the house was not attracting potential buyers, and why she always felt extremely uncomfortable when she was in the old place. Perhaps today the poltergeist with a penchant for untidiness has moved on to a less active eternity.

Trespassers Beware

The following story involves the mysterious deaths of two lifelong residents of The Pas. The fact that it was relayed by a retired RCMP officer, a man well familiar with investigating crime scenes, lends considerably credence to its authenticity as a paranormal killing. After all, you or I, in our shock at discovering grisly remains, might reasonably be expected to miss some important clues, but a career police officer has both the training and experience necessary to assess such a situation accurately.

The incident I refer to took place in the 1970s when this mountie was stationed in The Pas. He and his wife loved it there, feeling that it was one of the few, true frontiers left in this modern era. Inevitably, the police officer became friends with many of the residents. One man, Norm Duncan, he particularly admired. Unfortunately, Duncan's son David shared few of his father's admirable qualities. The young man was a ne'er do well, in trouble more often than he was out of it. And, as is often the case, his father was blind to much of his son's behaviour and defensive of what he did acknowledge. By the time David had nearly killed a man in a drunken brawl, even his long-suffering father knew there was nothing but grief ahead unless the young man changed his ways—radically.

It was late fall and in an effort to distract Dave from the only things he seemed to know how to do in town—drinking and fighting—Norm took his son to a cabin around Deer Lake where the older man planned to spend the winter trapping. As the father and son would be isolated from the rest of the world all winter, this was a serious commitment for both of them. Norm, understandably, took Dave's willingness to accompany him as an indication that his son was ready to be clear of his past, and that he was as anxious as everyone else in town to start his life over, on a considerably more positive note.

The two set off and were not heard from again until the following spring, when Norm was seen entering the police station. The Mountie listened as Norm recounted a successful trapping season and described in detail his trapline locations near the Saskatchewan River.

Despite the snow that had begun to fall, the pair had wasted no time setting up the traps: Norm looking after the line running southeast and Dave depositing a series of traps along the river bank. Several days later, they made their first trek out to check their catches. That evening the older man returned to the cabin with a respectable number of pelts while Dave returned empty-handed.

"What happened?" the father inquired.

"I'm not sure," Dave answered before launching into an angry tirade. He'd apparently seen lots of animal tracks but his traps were as empty as the day he'd laid them out. "I'm sure someone's stealing our furs. I just can't figure out how they're doing it because the only human tracks I saw the whole day were mine. Still, what else but a thief could explain the fact that there were animal tracks yet not a single catch?"

As he spoke and reviewed the situation in his mind, the younger man was becoming more agitated. "I saw smoke coming from a clearing across the river bank. It must have been coming from the thieving trapper's camp. I'm going over there tomorrow and have it out with him."

Although Norm certainly agreed that something would have to be done, he tried to talk his son into taking a more reasoned approach sensing that the younger man's temper was about to re-create, here in the bush, exactly the difficulties that had caused everyone so much trouble in town. Norm accompanied his son the next day, not trusting that his advice about calmer heads would be fully taken to heart.

They paddled their way through a circuitous part of the Saskatchewan River, parallel to where the still-empty traps lay. Sure enough, not far from the opposite shore, just where Dave had spotted smoke the day before, stood a decrepit cabin. They beached their canoe and before Norm could stop him, Dave was pounding on the cabin door.

As aggressive a young man as he was by nature, his anger at the thought of having been robbed, weakened his self-control even further. As the door to the lean-to opened, Dave Duncan prepared himself to do battle in any way necessary. The sight that met his angry gaze, however, stole his thunder completely. There, staring back at him, stood a native man so frail and elderly that he could not possibly have been responsible for stealing the catches from Dave's line. By this time his father had caught up with him and the two men could only gawk.

Dave found his voice first but rather than attacking the man either verbally or physically, he merely demanded to know whether or not the old man had been the one who had stolen from the trapline set up around the river.

The native elder slowly shook his head from side to side. When he spoke he assured the pair that he hadn't gone anywhere near their traps, nor would he ever—for the land on which Dave Duncan had laid those empty traps was hallowed.

"Many of my people are buried in that area. Their ghosts guard the place. You will never be able to hunt or trap successfully there. The spirits will not permit it. You must respect the land," the man pronounced slowly and quietly, before closing the door and receding into the darkness of his tiny residence.

The two men stood side-by-side staring at the closed door. Dave finally turned to his father and angrily said, "What a bunch of hocus pocus. He's just telling us that to scare us away from a good trapping spot."

"That may be so but somehow I don't think so. That man's too old to be lugging pelts around and besides, there was something very sincere about him. Frankly, Dave, I think he was telling the truth—that he really was trying to give us a warning. Let's just work the other line this season. There'll be more than enough for us there anyway."

To Norm's surprise, his son appeared to listen to him and, for once, to accept his father's advice.

"Didn't he seem odd to you?" the younger man asked rhetorically as they walked away from the ramshackle structure.

"You're right, he's not in good enough condition to be clearing traps so what's he living on way out there in the bush and why is he even there so far away from his people? There haven't been natives around these parts for years."

"I agree, it would be difficult for such an old man to survive under those circumstances but he was obviously managing adequately. I certainly didn't get any feeling that he needed help in any way. Quite the reverse. I don't think I've ever met anyone before who seemed that calm and serene."

The father and son made their way back to the cabin, still talking about who the elderly man might have been, what could account for his apparent serenity and how he would manage to keep body and soul together during winter.

Throughout the long cold season, the two men hauled in pelt after pelt from the trapline—the one that led straight to the southeast. At first they occasionally spoke of the old man but soon the strange interaction was all but forgotten. By spring the Duncans had harvested so many furs that their boat would not hold the entire catch and both men.

"You go ahead with the furs," Dave told his father. "I'll wait here until I can walk out. I'll meet you back in town in a few weeks."

Unwilling at first to accept such an arrangement, Norm finally had to admit that his son's plan might be the only one that would work. Once they had the pelts loaded onto the boat, they knew the decision had been the right one. The trapping had been so good that there simply wasn't room for both men in the boat.

After reminding Dave to stay away from the area they'd been told was sacred, Norm set off for The Pas, fully expecting to see his son again in just a few weeks. When the expected number of weeks doubled and then turned into months, Norm Duncan paid a call to the police station. He explained the circumstances under which his son was missing and advised the mountie that he was going back to the bush to look for Dave.

Now the native culture, of course, is filled with stories and legends of spirits and apparitions, but the culture to which both Norm Duncan and the police officer, listening to his concerns, belonged tended not to take such tales too seriously. For this reason, they looked for very different explanations to account for Dave Duncan's failure to show up as planned.

"Perhaps he's taken a job somewhere and not let you know," the officer reasoned.

Norm agreed that the idea was a possibility and so delayed a few days before heading out on his search. By then, however, he had become worried enough that, no matter how hard he tried to dismiss them, thoughts of the ghosts from the ancient burial ground somehow harming his son kept troubling him. He needed to find out for himself exactly what, if anything, had happened. He set out as soon as he could, letting the mountie know where he was headed and when he expected to return.

Weeks past and nothing was heard from either of the Duncans. Eventually, when even the older man's return to town was well overdue the officer decided he would have to take some action. After clearing the trip with his commanding officer, the mountie headed out in a float plane to find out what he could about the fate of the father-and-son trapping team. He arranged for the pilot to return in a few days to pick him up.

Just metres from where the plane had left him at the shore, the policeman recognized Norm Duncan's boat tied up at the shore near the cabin that he presumed also belonged to the missing man. The cabin was empty and had the same abandoned look to it that the beached boat had. The rust on the metal parts of the boat and the thickness of dust within the cabin told the searcher that neither had been touched in some weeks.

Not knowing what else to do, the officer got into the boat and, although he wasn't able to get the outboard motor started, between the current and the one paddle on board he made his way slowly down the shore looking for signs that either of the missing men might have been there, or with luck, still be there.

Finally, growing impatient with his search from the water, the Mountie decided to go ashore. Despite the fact that the terrain was not rough nor was the day overly warm, the policeman was soon sweating and feeling very uncomfortable. He came across the remains of an old lean-to in the woods but clearly no one had lived in there for a while—certainly not during the previous winter. The RCMP officer, who had been specially trained to look for clues, continued his search, all the while feeling less and less comfortable despite there being no real indication of anything to fear. There was absolutely no sign of recent human habitation anywhere in the area.

Despite his increasingly strong feelings of discomfort, by now verging on impending doom, the concerned officer knew he'd have to solve the mystery. He headed back to the boat and maneuvered it to the opposite shore, where he headed for the highest point he could find to have as clear as possible a vantage point and an opportunity to look around the area. There seemed to have been a severe fire through the bush in the past year but at first there were no signs that humans, the Duncans or anyone else, had been there.

Then the policeman's trained eyes spotted an anomaly—a birch tree, with its branches stripped and something bright red, something clearly not of nature, hanging from it. He scrambled down to investigate, hoping that he hadn't seen what he'd feared he'd seen. By now the intense feelings of discomfort he'd been feeling were manifesting themselves physically. The hair on the back of his neck was standing up. Goosebumps covered his arms and legs.

Scrambling down the slope towards the birch, he knew what he'd find. Still, the sight of what remained of Dave Duncan threw the man's stomach into knots. Obviously, the young man had been hanged for many months. By now the elements and the animals that had been at the body meant that nothing remained except a few bones caught up in the bits of cloth still attached to the tree.

At least now he knew where Dave Duncan was but it took him some time to figure out what had happened to the young man. It wasn't until he had been sitting and thinking for a few minutes that he remembered a native elder telling him that the tribe's ancestors once snared animals by building traps that hung from trees. Dave must have stumbled onto one of them. That hypothesis really didn't make sense, though, for the natives' trapping methods were, by now, well advanced from that method, and young Duncan couldn't have happened by an ancient, forgotten trap; it would have been so very old that the materials it had originally been made with would have rotted and disintegrated long ago. Besides, there hadn't been any native peoples in these woods for many years.

Getting up to pace, hoping the slight activity would help to clear his head and perhaps think more clearly, the Mountie made a second gruesome find. Not far from the foot of the tree lay the remains of a man's boot—a boot he recognized immediately as having belonged to Norm Duncan. As soon as he saw it, the Mountie knew he'd arrived weeks too late to help either father or son, for there was a gash clear through the boot. The man had come across his son's remains hanging in the tree. There was nothing the father could have done to have saved young David for he had been hanging there, dead, for many weeks by then. Still, of course, he'd have wanted to cut the corpse down and bring it back to town to give the lad a final and proper resting place.

Oddly, though, from the looks of the badly cut boot, Norm had missed when he'd swung his axe and instead of cutting through the brittle rawhide, the man had cut right through his own foot. From that blow on, he could do nothing but wait for the inevitable to happen. Norm Duncan must have known that out in the bush by himself he would soon bleed to death. Hoping that the end was swift for both Dave and his father, the Mountie did the only thing he could have done under the circumstances—he buried what remained of both men in such a way that their graves would likely never be discovered.

The plane wouldn't be back to take the police officer home to The Pas until the following day so he tried to make himself as comfortable as he could throughout the night. Sleep was impossible because, although there was no apparent danger from the surrounding wilderness, the man felt a strong but free-floating sense of a threat around him.

The next morning he put the axe he'd found at the scene in the Duncans' long-beached boat and pushed it out into the current. By then there was nothing to do but wait for his ride home. What a welcome sight that plane must have been as it flew over the horizon. The man told his pilot that he'd found the Duncans' cabin deserted. He also suggested that before they flew out of the area, it might be wise to do a few low-altitude circles around the river, the lake and the land surrounding them. On the second fly past, they spotted an overturned boat that the Mountie identified as looking like one that Norm Duncan owned. The pilot immediately suggested that the pair had lost control going over the rapids and apparently drowned. The policeman only said that he couldn't think of a more reasonable explanation.

From there the matter was pretty much dropped. It was many years before the man could speak to anyone of his experiences by Deer Lake and when he did he only told the story once. This was one double murder that was never recorded in police files.

Visiting Mystics Host Seances

Considering Winnipeg was virtually the birthplace of rational psychic research, with Dr. Hamilton's world-famous experiments (see p. 69), the opening sentence of a short article in the August 23, 1938, edition of the *Winnipeg Free Press* is rather odd. "Winnipeg people just don't seem to be interested in psychic phenomena." The mediums' reported disappointment with the size of the crowds they attracted, however, seems to me to be contradicted by the information given in the body of the article. Here, newspaper readers are informed that a group of fifty individuals paid a dollar to attend the seance given by psychics who had travelled from southern Ontario and the province of Quebec.

Shortly after the crowd had assembled, two of the psychics went into a trance. Almost immediately, the room was filled with a ghostly sound. One of the people present was a Mr. W.R. Wood, a former Member of the Legislative Assembly and an admirer of the recently deceased Dr. Hamilton. He asked the spirit to identify itself and was likely not surprised to find that the ghost of T.G. Hamilton was paying a call. Although Wood tried to communicate with Hamilton's ghost, the results were weak and the spirit soon lost the strength needed to continue to be present with the living.

Although disappointed to lose contact with a pioneer in the field of paranormal study, the crowd was soon fascinated by a metal trumpet that floated about the room, seemingly of its own accord. The instrument, reported to be about a metre in length, stopped near individuals for whom the spirits had messages and occasionally emitted sighs and apparent attempts to gain breath.

Suspiciously, the seance was not over until all present had received messages from beyond. Such consistency would make anyone, skeptic or believer, wonder if the seance hadn't been a carefully orchestrated hoax and, in part, it might have been. Conversely, anyone who has ever been involved in an attempt to summon spirits will tell you that it is not, in fact, very difficult: a group of people focusing their energy towards that end will almost always provoke a supernatural reaction. It is also extremely likely that some of the ghostly visitors to the room that evening had welcomed the opportunity to transcend their plane and send messages to their loved ones left behind here on earth.

If the visiting mystics were truly disappointed by the results of that late summer sitting in 1938, you'd have to wonder exactly how they measured success.

Phone-in Phantoms

Ghost stories that are told to me on radio show phone-in programs almost always support this premise: a true ghost story has a fragmented quality to it that a work of fiction never has. To add to this tendency towards fragmentation, I think callers are somewhat uncomfortable sharing such a personal experience through such a public medium.

Just before the Halloweens of both 1995 and 1996, Bill Turner with CKLQ Radio in Brandon invited me to join him on air. Both visits were experiences that certainly supported my aforementioned theory. People gave admittedly condensed versions of their stories despite the fact that I had asked everyone to please take a few minutes and jot me a quick note fleshing out the details. Only one person ever did. As a result, what we have here is a collection of tantalizingly abbreviated true Manitoba ghost stories.

The first caller in 1995 had two provocative tales to tell. Both were about his grandfather's ghost. The first took place just a week after the older man's funeral.

"It was a Friday night and my mother and myself were sitting in the living room watching television," the man began before explaining that he had enjoyed an exceptionally close relationship with his grandfather. "Suddenly, we smelled perked coffee."

The man and his mother ran to the kitchen where they had left a Pyrex coffee pot on the stove set up and ready to be perked for breakfast the next morning.

"The coffee pot was boiling but the element was stone cold," he asserted.

The caller went on to explain that when he removed the pot from the cold element and set it to the side, the phenomenon ceased. Undeniably intriguing but what made him think that his was a ghost story and why did he tie it in with his beloved grandfather's recent death? After all, he'd said nothing about his house being haunted nor had he connected the impromptu coffee party in any way with the older man.

Seconds later, however, he tied it all together most effectively with the simple statement, "Grandad loved perked coffee."

The gentleman's next story took place some months later.

"Mom used to grow roses. Grandad lived about eight or nine houses from us and he used to like to walk down to our house and see the flowers. In the fall when the roses were finished, my mother would take them out of the garden and put them in the back lane [for disposal]," the caller asserted.

This year the routine turned out to be a little different from what it had been the previous years. The roses that she'd removed from her garden because they were dying off lay next to the back alley for several days—in full and glorious bloom.

No doubt the coffee-drinking, flower-loving ghost of Grandad wanted everyone, himself included, to enjoy the roses' beauty just a few days longer.

The next caller, a woman, quickly admitted what her somewhat hesitant voice had already revealed. "I'm a little bit nervous," she stated simply. Her ghost story was slightly different than any I'd ever heard before.

"My story's a little bit different," she began. "It took place several years ago when I was a teenager."

The young woman went on to explain that at the time she belonged to the Mormon religion. Tradition in that church dictates that a person can offer themselves as a stand-in for a deceased person in need of baptism. Many times, the caller told us, she agreed to take part in these ceremonies.

"I've been baptized for about seventy people," she said.

Whenever she participated in the ritual she "could feel somebody there beside me." The caller always presumed that it was the spirit of the person in whose name she was being baptized that she could sense alongside her.

The caller further explained that the presence she felt was always a female one, and that fits with the ceremony as tradition deems that you are only baptized in the name of someone of your own gender.

The next caller was a gentleman who began by saying, "I've always been fascinated by the possibility of ghosts but I never had an experience until I worked for a travel trailer company in Winnipeg. The company had a house on the property that was used for the office. One night I was alone in the house and I heard footsteps. I was quite surprised but I wasn't scared at first. I just thought there was someone in the house."

After a thorough check, he realized he was as alone as he'd originally thought he was and that the sounds he'd heard were actually phantom footsteps. The caller told us that he immediately felt uncomfortable and fled the house.

Because he was employed by the company that owned the apparently haunted house, a second encounter with the invisible resident was inevitable. But by then the man had discerned that the spirit meant him no harm. From then on, when he heard the ghost walking about, he stayed, finished whatever business he had to attend to and actually felt comforted by the presence of his paranormal companion.

"There was an aura in the house that made you feel there was someone with you. I felt it was an older male. It was a very comfortable feeling," he reiterated. "I was only frightened that first time. Once I took someone else with me and they heard it, too. It was an exciting feeling, but comforting."

Of course, the man was curious about what ghost was walking about the house-cum-office, but he had no efficient way of finding out. By now it is too late.

"It was an older home, built in the 1920s. It's since been destroyed."

Perhaps the spirit has moved on either to another earthly abode or to somewhere even better.

The first caller to the 1996 phone-in show was a man whose story had a very familiar theme to it. Many stories I've heard over the years support the theory that certain houses are haunted by something or someone unpleasant and that these negative presences are so strong they can actually have a detrimental effect on the well-being of a family unfortunate enough to move into such a house.

The gentleman explained that over the years he has lived in a number of rented houses in four Canadian provinces. While determining whether or not a particular house would be right for his family, this man took more into account than merely size and location.

"I always go by the feel of the house. Some houses are friendly and some aren't."

By using this intuitive process, the man had determined, "There are good houses and bad houses."

Sadly, he proved his theory even to himself.

"My wife and I are divorced now but [years ago] we were renting a house. We had ten years of a great marriage."

The couple had children and the youngsters were apparently very enthusiastic about the possibility of the family purchasing a house rather than just renting one.

"Finally, we bought a house ... One of the kids really wanted a room in the basement," the man recalled.

Because his parents could accommodate such a request with the newly purchased home, the child was thrilled when the family finally made the move. Despite his initial enthusiasm for his basement bedroom, "Every morning he'd end up in his brother's bedroom [upstairs]."

Too bad the parents didn't understand that the child's behaviour was caused by a ghostly presence in their home.

"The kids were irritable the whole time we lived there. The personality of the entire family changed," he added. So much so that in spite of the long and healthy relationship the caller and his wife had when they moved into the house, they were soon divorced.

"When the marriage split up, my wife and kids went to live in Kelowna. I stayed on but rented the house out. The renters said they saw images of little kids [in the house]. Eventually, I sold it [and] about six months later the house was torn down."

Sadly, the haunted house had already done permanent damage to the once-happy family.

"We never did manage to get back together, but we're friends now."

Presumably the caller has long since gone back to letting the "feel" of a place determine whether or not he moves into it.

The next phone call was from a woman who explained that a number of years ago a favourite uncle had died. As the caller was in the hospital at the time of the funeral, she thought she'd lost her last chance to say a final good-bye and pay her last respects to a man she knew fondly.

Her fear, however, turned out to be unfounded. Because she wasn't able to go to her uncle, he came to her.

"The night of the funeral I had a dream and I saw my uncle with a whole bunch of relatives that I'd never met and a little boy about three years old. The little boy told me he was my Uncle Johnny. He told me that he was my guardian angel and that he's kept me safe and now he's keeping my daughters safe, too."

The information revealed in the dream wasn't entirely a surprise to the caller as she'd known that in the previous generation there had been a little boy who'd died as a toddler.

The final caller began by telling us that he did believe in ghosts. After he'd explained his experiences that first piece of information wasn't really very surprising.

"My wife and I smell cigar smoke in the house at nights and

[another smell] like someone [is] cooking bacon and eggs and making toast. This happens anywhere between 2:00 a.m. and 4:00 a.m."

Just in case anyone might think either the caller or his wife were experiencing olfactory hallucinations, he went on to describe an event that occurred when they had guests staying at their home overnight.

"My son-in-law woke up and smelled toast. He was going to get up and have toast with whomever was up ... but decided not to. The next morning he asked which one of them was up eating. Of course, no one was," the caller recalled and then added, "We call him Charlie our ghost. We decided he just wanted a friend and was hungry and so we just let him eat."

Charlie doesn't visit every night. "On different nights my wife and I would smell the different smells."

But what of the cigar smoke? That apparently was consistent. "Old Port cigars," the man stated emphatically.

On Halloween morning in 1997, I received what has come to be an expected, and extremely welcome, phone call from Bill Turner, of CKLQ radio in Brandon. Just like the past couple of Halloweens, the two of us spent the next hour on his live radio show chatting with some of his many listeners—specifically those who had Manitoba ghost stories to tell.

The first man to call reported that the Memorial Hall in Carberry was haunted. It had been a drill hall and apparently, to date, not all of the soldiers have left the old building. While a theatre company prepared for a show there, the members were aware of a presence, and two previous caretakers have reported that they routinely heard the distinctive sounds of marching feet—despite the fact that they were alone in the building at the time. One of these two men also heard a loud sneeze and although he checked the building over completely he found no source for the sound.

That last observation leads one to wonder whether we carry our viruses or allergies to the great beyond.

The next caller began by telling Bill and me that he would not believe in ghosts, "if it weren't for the strange goings-on" that he'd been witness to over the years. He explained that the history of this particular haunting goes back to the early 1950s.

Apparently, as a young wife, the caller's mother would hear disembodied footsteps around the house when her husband was working night shifts. As the years went by, the family became accustomed to the sounds but then, more recently, the stereo in the house began acting strangely. The volume would go up and down, even though no one was near the machine. Eventually, the family determined that its invisible visitor was the caller's paternal great-grandfather. The older man died when his grandson was only thirteen. The two had been very close, and as a result the man who'd called to tell us the story said he never felt frightened by the ghost of his great-grandfather, rather he always felt protected by it.

The third caller, also a man, began the conversation with the simple and yet profound statement: "I believe we have spirits." He went on to describe the sourceless, cool drafts throughout his residence before adding that his daughter has heard unexplainable music in the house. He also spoke of a time when every wind-up clock in the house was reading the same time. Not so unusual you might think, except that all the clocks were reading exactly ten minutes slow.

The caller took one of the clocks into work with him that day, intending to investigate the problem. He didn't explain whether or not he had a chance to take the mechanism apart, but he did report that the electrical clock at his place of employment suddenly and inexplicably also read ten minutes slow.

The man wonders if the odd occurrence with the timepieces was in any way connected to two old portraits in a bedroom in his house. He reported that they were "the old-fashioned kind where the eyes followed you." His grandchildren reacted with great fright to the paintings and could not be persuaded to sleep in the room while the pictures were there. As soon as they were removed, the children fell contentedly asleep.

The only woman to call the show that Friday in 1997 also had a theory about where her ghost might have come from. The house she referred to is located near a main railway line. She has long been convinced that there is an occasional presence in the house. By now she's become so used to the entity that she has taken to speaking to it when she feels it's nearby. The caller speculates that the spirit she feels could somehow be connected to the railway. She thinks he might have died while riding the rails, possibly during the Depression, and that he is only looking, in death, for something that eluded him in life—a place to rest.

The woman is not the only one in her family to be aware of the entity. When her niece stayed overnight, the child complained that she couldn't get to sleep because the woman's cat was making so much noise walking around. At the time the little girl made that statement, the cat was curled up, asleep at the end of the caller's bed.

"Are they angels or are they ghosts?" the next gentleman wondered before adding that the following incidents were "true and happened to us."

Twenty years before, the man and his wife had lived in a small town. They'd "always hear movement upstairs" even though no one was there. The next incident occurred after the couple bought a pair of candle holders at a rummage sale. They set them out as a decoration, but the ornaments would never stay where they were put.

Whatever was in the house possessed a love of radio in common with many other ghosts. When the radio was on, the spirit would turn it off. When it was off, it would turn on. This ghost's love of music extended to the piano, which the couple heard being played. They had thought they were alone in the house and when they went to check as to whom the pianist might have been, the music stopped and they found the room as empty as they'd expected it to be. Despite no one being around, the lid to the piano keys had been opened, which was not the way the instrument had been left.

The man theorized that the long-deceased former owner of the house might have been responsible for the initial haunting. However, since then his wife has died and he's suspicious that her spirit might still be near him. At times when he is in the bedroom he has observed a dim light coming from the living room. "It was like a half burned-out light, dim and dark," but apparently still a noticeable illumination.

"Another night I saw [a similar] light from the kitchen. When I said 'hello' the light went dim," he described.

The next time he saw the light, it was again in the kitchen. This time he went into the room that was so oddly lit. He described seeing a shadow of a figure there before emphasizing that the light was not from an electrical source.

By now the vision of the strange light and shadow have become routine in the man's house, and he's completely comfortable with the phenomenon. He closed the conversation by assuring Bill and me, "Nothing scares me."

The last caller of the day was also a man and he had quite a story to tell. Years ago, he and his wife bought a small house. Rather than moving into the place right away, the man explained, they "tore the house down to ground level." They intended to use the original foundation after raising it about three feet. This change, the couple reasoned, would give their new house a high basement ceiling. Little did they suspect what else the alterations would bring them.

While working around the property, the man reported that he'd begun chatting with people in the neighbourhood. He'd learned, among other things, that the previous owner had recently died—in the front bedroom.

"I asked [the neighbour] not to say anything to my wife about that because we were planning to put our bedroom in that corner of the [re-built] house and if she knew about the man's death she'd be seeing things for sure."

The reconstruction went smoothly and the couple moved into their new home on the old foundation. They lived there happily and the neighbour kept her word about not relating the circumstances of the former owner's death to the caller's wife. Despite this secrecy, the man's hunch proved to be correct—his wife was "seeing things."

The woman kept her thoughts to herself for a while but finally informed her husband that, "There's a ghost in the bedroom." The man listened as his wife described the consistent pattern she'd been observing: a very small man, roughly three feet in height, would walk around the couple's dresser before simply disappearing from view.

There wasn't much question as to whom the apparition was, but his small stature puzzled the owners of this new house. They'd understood that the man who'd lived for many years in the house they'd torn down had been of normal height. After giving the confusing matter considerable thought, they remembered that an important part of the re-building process had been raising the level of the foundation. This, of course, had given them the increased head room in the basement that they'd wanted but, of course, it had also raised the level of the main floor. Their bedroom was in the same location as the previous owner's had been, but their new floor was nearly three feet higher than the old one.

Once they had put all of this information together, the couple realized that the ghost was the owner of the demolished house and that he was simply carrying on his familiar routines—on the floor that existed when he existed.

Now that's as varied and fascinating a collection of phone-in ghost stories as anyone could ever want.

The Haunted Plains

Places where great trauma has been suffered are very likely to be haunted. In Alberta, at the site of the Frank Slide—where an entire town was practically buried by an early morning rockslide in 1903—even today people report seeing eerie shapes and shadows moving among still-strewn boulders. In the United States, ghosts of Civil War soldiers are still seen battling on into their eternity. And here in Manitoba, apparitions are occasionally reported at the site of a deadly conflict between rival tribes in Portage La Prairie.

On a cold winter's day, an undisclosed number of Assiniboines were headed home from an Ojibway pow-wow, which had been held in the Lake of the Woods area. As they made their way across the Portage Plains, the travellers were ambushed by a Cree war party who had watched the Assiniboines as the group advanced. The Assiniboines were not only caught completely off guard but were at an even more serious disadvantage, because they were suffering the effects of having consumed far too much of their hosts' liquid hospitality.

The battle was short and tragic. None of the Assiniboines lived to tell the tale. Their bodies were hastily buried at the site of the massacre and forgotten. The trauma of the assault, however, has succeeded in scarring the psychic landscape in a way similar to that reported of the Civil War battles, for to this day strange and unexplainable figures are seen in the area.

One man reported that he had been badly shaken from an experience he had on the Portage Plains, very near the native burial ground. It was winter, and as he walked through the freshly fallen snow he saw the image of a person off in the distance. Concerned that someone might be lost or in some other way in need of assistance, the man made his way over to where he'd seen the image. When he got there, not only was the area vacant but there were not even any tracks in the snow. Despite this evidence to the contrary, he was still sure that he had seen a person.

Further investigation of the area and the lore surrounding the area finally convinced the man that what he had seen had not actually been a human being but an apparition—presumably the ghost of a slain and disgraced Assiniboine warrior.

The Legend of the White Horse

Approximately 160 kilometres east of Brandon, near St. Francois Xavier, at the junction of the Trans-Canada Highway and Highway 26, stands an imposing statue—the statue of a white horse. Manitoba historian Bonnie Robbins explained the statue was a monument, "erected to preserve one of the oldest legends in Manitoba."

The story goes that a Sioux brave longed to make a certain Assiniboine maiden his bride. The young woman was the chief's daughter. The father refused the Sioux's request and, instead, granted his daughter in marriage to a Cree chief—a man who had promised to give the Assiniboine tribe a snow-white horse as a "thank-you" gift. The selfish father did not move quickly enough, however, and before the maiden's marriage to the Cree took place she and the young warrior ran off together, escaping on the white steed that had been the Cree chief's gift.

When the father of the bride and her betrothed discovered that the woman, her lover and the stallion were gone, the men were furious. Tragically, the couple were hunted down and killed but the horse that had been carrying them to freedom managed to make good his escape. For years after, the steed's ghost could be seen galloping across the White Horse Prairie.

A rather interesting addendum exists regarding the roadside statue that commemorates the ghostly legend. It was apparently paid for by a company that distills scotch whisky and features a similar steed on its label.

The statue of the white horse is a tribute to an old Manitoba legend.

A Terrifying Spirit

The culture of Canadian native peoples is quite accepting of the concept of phantoms. One particularly fearful spirit acknowledged within the native culture is known as a "Weetigo." (There are roughly three dozen ways to spell this name; all begin with "W" and are three syllables in length.) These entities sometimes inhabit bodies of live persons, causing the person to perform terrible feats that they otherwise would not have committed. Cannibalism, as an example, is one of the frequently ascribed unspeakably evil acts performed by the Weetigo.

Weetigos do not, however, have to find a living body to host their return visit to earth. They can also take the form of a giant apparition, described as being "as tall as a spruce tree" and having a black face without lips.

A particularly frightening sighting of this nature was reported in the August 1, 1952, edition of the *Winnipeg Free Press.* The spirit was said to be in the form of a giant woman "who presses her face against the window pane of the cabin at night and watches." Neither a date nor a location were given for the appearance of this ghostly peeping Thomasina.

As frightening as such a phantom sighting must have been, even worse stories pre-date that one. Another Weetigo, this one possessing the ability to fly, was said to be responsible for the disappearance of two trappers one winter.

After Chief Henry Fiddler spotted one of the Weetigo spirits approaching, he posted a sign on his door warning of the apparition's presence and moved his people out of the spirit's way. The seriousness of the threat was reported to be such that

"Even the picture show was poorly attended," according to Beth Paterson writing in the *Winnipeg Free Press* on August 1, 1952.

The Weetigo's arrival in an area was always deeply dreaded, not only for its own fearful sake, but because such sightings were frequently associated with illness and death. More stories of the strange Weetigo follow.

Although the following story is a very old one by Canadian standards, if it had happened exactly where it did, but just four years earlier, the events would have happened in Manitoba. Let me explain.

More than a century ago, there was a small settlement nestled in the southeast corner of the province. Geographically, the hamlet was an attractive one but whomever named the place certainly didn't do so with an eye to public appeal, for he chose the moniker "Rat Portage." Despite its odd name, the Manitoba community flourished until 1892 when an interprovincial boundary dispute caused the area surrounding Rat Portage to fall under the auspices of the province of Ontario. The story that follows didn't take place until 1896 but because of the town's Manitoba heritage (to say nothing of that intriguing piece of demographic and historical trivia), it was deemed to be suitable for re-telling in his book.

On December 7, 1896, a short article appeared in the *Winnipeg Free Press*. The date line was three days prior and the write-up reported on a tragic court case that had taken place in Rat Portage on December 3 of that year. It seems that for some time previously the Sabaskong in the area had been terrified by the presence of a Weetigo. The Weetigo was appearing in human form—what we would understand today as an apparition.

The natives were convinced that the ghostly presence threatened the tribe's well-being and that, in fact, it had already harmed some of their property. The band tried hiding from the

Weetigo but apparently to no avail. Finally, in an attempt to protect themselves from further harm, the band set up a system of round-the-clock watches.

On the eighth night of the watch, one of the guards saw a mysterious figure flitting from one spot to another, with its blanket streaming behind it in a peculiar manner. He fired at what he was firmly convinced was the Weetigo. In the yell that followed, the [guard] recognized the voice of his foster father, who, for some reason or another, had left his post and was probably hastening back to it.

The young guard would have been hailed as a hero among his people if the figure had been the roaming spirit. Now, tragically, the guard stood charged with the murder of the man who had raised him. The judge, Mr. Justice Rose, was faced with presiding over a trial for which there was no precedent. After hearing arguments from Crown Attorney Langford rebutted by defence attorney Wink, the jury brought in a decision of guilty—of manslaughter which they deemed to be punishable by a term of six months' hard labour.

Given the leniency of the sentence for having taken the life of another, it is clear that the court recognized that the man firmly believed he was firing at an evil ghost and not a live person. The implications are indeed fascinating.

And as for the one-time Manitoba hamlet of Rat Portage, whatever happened to the unattractively named community? Given that few of us would ever have heard of Rat Portage perhaps, like many early Canadian towns, its population diminished over time until it became deserted—a ghost town. While that would be a logical assumption, in this case it would not be a correct one.

The town that used to be known as Rat Portage, Manitoba eventually became Kenora, Ontario. The last two letters of the name "Kenora" are the only reminders of the original name—the town where one man shot another man having mistaken him for an evil ghost. The word "Kenora" is made up of the first two letters of the names of the surrounding communities: Keewatin, Norman and Rat Portage.

Judging from the reports I've found, when Manitoba lost Rat Portage they did not lose all the Weetigo stories. Late in January, 1934, RCMP Sergeant Percy Rose was dispatched by dogsled to investigate strange reports. Grisly ghost stories had filtered out to the towns and cities further south from native settlements at Burntwood Bay and Reindeer Lake, near the Northwest Territories' border. The gist of the stories was that a Weetigo, or cannibal spirit, had inhabited a young brave's body. Unable to deal with this frightening and uncontrollable entity, the tribe tied the man to a dogsled and left him to freeze to death. Presumably once the body the Weetigo had implanted itself in was dead, the spirit would vanish.

That much of the story made the front page of the day's newspaper, but I was unable to locate any follow-up article. One hopes that this lack of news was because the officer's trek was uneventful, that he found order restored in the tribe and that he returned to his post without incident. I stress that is what we can sincerely hope happened. There is always the fear, however, that the bodiless Weetigo, searching for a new host, spotted the policeman on his dogsled and the officer was then never heard from again. A chilling possibility.

In 1907, Pe-Oe-Quan, an elderly native shaman, was rumoured to be responsible for killing twenty people in his tribe. He was apparently sure that each one of the twenty had been haunted by the Weetigo. Although the native justice system seemed to accept this situation, the "white man's" system was appalled by it and promptly charged the old man with murder. Although Pe-Oe-Quan hanged himself before the police were able to apprehend him, the law enforcers did arrest the tribal chief, a man named Mistainnew, who had also been implicated in the deaths. Mistainnew was tried, convicted and sentenced to Stony Mountain penitentiary where he eventually died.

The Lost Soul

There are few places in the world as ethnically diverse as Manitoba. It wasn't much of a surprise, then, when writer Nancy Bennett, who grew up in Manitoba, explained that the province is home to at least one immigrant spirit, of sorts. She tells it this way.

The Mori are ghosts of the Icelandic people. Sometime around 1900, an Icelander turned his back on his people and journeyed to Canada to start a new life. He settled in Manitoba. Once his people learned that the man was not coming home, they raised the spirit of the Mori to track him down and haunt him.

But the Mori was used to Icelandic terrain. Soon the poor spirit was lost and unable to find either the victim he was to haunt or his own way home. This Mori is said to be very lonely but also very shy. He is dressed all in brown and you might catch a glimpse of him out of the corner of your eye.

Occasionally, he will knock at a door in Manitoba looking for companionship, but he always leaves before anyone can answer. Nancy concludes her story by instructing anyone who happens to see the foreign ghost to tell him how to find his way home. "They say many Mori roam [in Iceland] and our lonely immigrant ghost would feel more at home with his otherworld companions."

Ignis Fatuus/Ghost Lights

Ghost lights are among the oldest reported paranormal phenomena. Stories of the luminescent apparitions exist in many cultures and date back to the earliest times. Although they are most commonly referred to as simply "ghost lights," they are also known by many other names. In her book *Ghost Stories of Saskatchewan*, author Jo-Anne Christensen explains that earth lights, phantom lights, will o' the wisp and *ignis fatuus* are all synonymous phrases for the "unexplained, elusive, luminescent globes of spectral fire that have fascinated people for centuries."

Christensen goes on to explain that although the Latin *ignis fatuus* translates to "foolish fire," "... there are those who take this 'foolishness' very seriously."

Just less than 150 kilometres south and east of Winnipeg, you'll find the small and somewhat isolated town of Woodridge. The town might not be a large cosmopolitan centre, but it does have pretty much everything a person would need, including, for at least the past sixty years anyway, a ghost. Because the phantom is closely connected with the railway and his origin pinned to the Depression era, locals suspect that he could have been one of the thousands of hobos riding the rails across Canada in search of work. It is presumed that he met an untimely and accidental death perhaps on the train tracks.

A member of the railway track maintenance crew was the first to notice the paranormal activity. The man, whose name has been lost to history, lived in a company-supplied house near the tracks just outside Woodridge. The exact location of the residence was just begging for a ghost. It was near an old woodland cemetery and had at one time been used as a church. It was a two-storey place with a toolshed in the form of a rough lean-to built against one side of it.

The first sign of a ghostly presence in the house was footsteps on the main floor when the worker and his family were all upstairs in their beds at night. Although one or other of the family members might have been able to sleep through the sounds of the entity walking, none of the family got even a wink of sleep on the nights he decided to hammer and rattle chains.

The presence didn't restrict himself to mere sounds, however. He even liked to play with marbles owned by the worker's son. We can only imagine the child's reaction as he stood and watched the marble collection, seemingly of its own accord, jump clear out of the jar in which they were stored.

The worker decided to search out and try to eliminate as many objects as possible that might be attractive noise- and nuisance-makers for the ghost the family now admitted they had. Some of what he tracked down and threw away made little or no difference but when he removed the ropes once used to lower coffins into the graves in the nearby cemetery, the poltergeist-like activity the family had been enduring was markedly reduced and only the nightly hammering continued.

The family lived in its haunted company-owned house for more than a decade before the ghost began to manifest himself in other ways. The worker's wife observed the supernatural sight. Early one winter evening as the woman was bringing laundry in from the clothesline, she looked up to see a form carrying an old-fashioned gas lantern. She watched in fascination as the ghost moved away from her and towards the remains of the old church nearby. She ran to tell her husband about the extraordinary sight and he immediately set out in search of the phantom. He found nothing—not even footsteps in the snow where his wife had clearly observed the apparition trekking.

But sightings of this particular ghost aren't restricted to members of this one family. Hunters in the area have reported seeing a man with a lantern following them. They reported that at those times, their normally brave and well-trained hunting dogs would run back to the hunters' truck at the edge of the wood and cower, hiding under the vehicle and refusing to be coaxed back out even to join their owners.

By now the long-deceased man is usually reduced to displaying his leftover energy merely in the form of a phantom light, although occasionally witnesses swear that they have heard an unearthly moaning. The light, however, has become a local institution with people driving out regularly to see if they will be treated to a glimpse of the ghostly glowing.

When it does appear, the ghost light has a predictable effect on power sources and receivers. Radios and cigarette lighters in cars fail to work while the light is visible because the batteries, which effectively power them before the light appears and after it disappears, are temporarily drained. This means that if you go out to the Woodridge area and see the light, you have to hope you're not frightened by it for you will be stuck right where you are until the light disappears. After all, your car won't start with a dead battery.

Fortunately, most who go to see the paranormal luminescence consider themselves privileged and are not interested in leaving before the show is over. When the light first appears, it is not only tiny but quite faint. Within a few minutes, it increases in both size and brilliance until it lights up the entire area. It has been reported that "it almost blinds you."

Interestingly, the Woodridge phantom light is not always white but can also appear as either a blue or a red glow and it can actually be quite aggressive—seeming to chase after people who've come to see it. As everyone who has had the experience of being chased by the peculiar apparition has successfully fled, no one knows what might happen if the ghost from the 1930s actually caught up with an observer.

The phantom light phenomenon is apparently intercultural. The following story was reported in *The Albertan*, a now-defunct paper from Calgary, Alberta.

On October 10, 1936, a headline in that paper proclaimed, "GHOSTLY LIGHT DANCES ACROSS WESTERN LAKE." The article goes on to describe "a peculiar light [which] floats back and forth, tantalizingly out of reach off the western shores of Lake Winnipeg."

Obviously at the time, the phenomena was considered interesting enough to be newsworthy to a non-native newspaper but despite this the piece then went on to describe the traditional Cree explanation for the mysterious light. "Legend describes it as the Lantern of Pale Moon, Cree Indian maiden who perished in a blizzard to keep a lover's tryst. When the will o' the wisp appears over the water, southwest of Berens Island, nervous [women] hurry children to their teepees, fearful of evil spirits."

In 1936, the time of this report, at least one elderly man, an Ojibway Chief named Skeet, survived who still remembered Pale Moon herself. He was just a youthful brave when Pale Moon met a young Scotsman, a fur trader, "who set his trapline in the upper reaches of the lake country." It was love at first sight and from then on the two made a point to see one another as frequently as they could throughout summer. As fall approached, the trapper received orders to return to his employer's trading post. He promised to come back to his beloved within a month.

Pale Moon waited patiently for the period of their separation to be over. On the first evening after the four weeks had passed, she took her lantern down to the shore in hopes of spotting his canoe paddling towards her. There was no sight of her Scottish lover that evening but she wasn't discouraged. She merely returned every evening at sundown, carrying her lantern to light her way and to guide his arrival safely ashore.

Night after night, the young woman made her pilgrimage, lantern in hand. Soon, the harsh winter set in and Pale Moon's family and friends tried to dissuade her from continuing her ritual. They worried about the once-pretty maiden. It was evident from the deterioration in her appearance that she had become worn by the routine and the unrewarded waiting.

Her vigil continued for fully a year until one exceptionally cold, stormy evening when she set out, trusty lantern in hand, on her regular, futile trek to the shore of Lake Winnipeg. This trip through the woods, however, was tragically different for she never returned to her home. In fact, Pale Moon was never seen again.

Her people were so distraught by Pale Moon's disappearance that they soon moved away from the area. Had Skeet not returned two years later to the shores of Lake Winnipeg as a guide, it is likely that no one would ever have connected the phantom light across the lake with the ghost of the woman. Skeet, however, made a point to search, at least, for clues as to what might have happened. His hunt was rewarded with a grisly find: two skeletons, one still clutching a lantern in her fingers.

To this day at the inlet 175 miles north of Winnipeg, on murky nights, Pale Moon's ghost can be seen waving her lantern to guide her lover to shore.

Not all ghost lights have this tranquil a nature, however. A Cree man, an employee of the Hudson's Bay Company, who identified himself as "O-GE-MAS-ES," which he translated as meaning "Little Clerk," told a terrifying tale of a menacing phantom light. The incident occurred a very long time ago, in the

1870s. (The other story involving Little Clerk can be found on p. 161.)

In the dead of winter, Little Clerk received word from his superiors that he was to leave his post on the shore of Lake Manitoba immediately in order to investigate reports from a native community across the lake. It seemed that an elderly native woman had become possessed by a presence and was a danger to those around her.

To fully appreciate the depth to which this man was frightened by his paranormal experience, it is important to understand Little Clerk's personality. Fortunately, through his long-windedness, the man left a clear impression of himself. He goes on at length about his team of four dogs, Herod, Nero, Hero and Moro, whom he reports were "part Esquimeaux and part wolf hound" and raves glowingly not only about their intelligence and courage but also about the depth of their devotion to him. These dogs apparently pulled the man's sleigh—a sleigh as extraordinary as the animals were themselves.

From reading his report one must assume that as a result of being so effectively and handsomely equipped to make the one hundred–kilometre trek across a frozen lake, Little Clerk "looked forward to the trip with enjoyment." And, at first anyway, enjoyment was apparently what he experienced, for fifty years after the trip he recorded that "While I lay back in my cariole, comfortably wrapped in furs the miles slipped by." Clearly, this Little Clerk was no complainer. Here was a man with an attitude so positive that, had there been such a character at the time, he could have given Mary Poppins a serious run for her money.

His mood, however, was about to take a dip. Little Clerk was about to have his first encounter with an entity. Although it was past sundown, it was a cloudless night and the sky was lit with not only the moon and stars but also the northern lights. Without warning, the man's tranquillity was disturbed by something he could neither see nor hear but rather only feel. He suddenly felt that he was not alone. He felt alarmed despite knowing full well that there could be no one except himself and his dogs within miles.

Like most of us would do, Little Clerk's immediate response to the uncomfortable feeling was to deny it to himself. For a few moments, he tried to tell himself he was only imagining things. After all, if what he was feeling was real, he would be forced to suddenly go from being relaxed and happy to being uncomfortable and in danger.

Sadly, the man's ability for denial was not equal to the task at hand, for not only did the distinct feeling of a presence stay, it actually grew stronger. Eventually, he had to admit he had a problem and sat up in his sleigh to assess the situation. There, beside his team, "dancing along" was "a ball of phosphorescent light."

Worse, the supernatural glow seemed to have a will of its own. It was "keeping pace with the dogs" and "kept changing size." One second the frightened Little Clerk reported that the light was "as large as a football and at others not much bigger than a cricket ball."

Once adjusted to his own feelings of fear, Little Clerk turned his attention to his four beloved dogs. As animals are usually more receptive to the presence of spirits than humans are, it is not surprising that they were reacting to the spirit light.

"Instead of swinging along in their usual free fashion with tails waving, they appeared cowed, and on my speaking to them and endeavouring to draw their attention to the luminous light and setting them on it, for the first time in their lives they paid no attention to me. ..."

Seriously distressed now both by the eerie light staying parallel to him and by his dogs' out-of-character behaviour, Little Clerk tried to grasp at least some control over the situation. He ordered his dogs to stop but they ignored his command. The man now realized that by spooking his dogs this way, the phantom light was actually posing a threat to his life. If the animals were either led or frightened away from their task, he would be stranded in the dark in the middle of the frozen lake.

The light responded to his fear by putting on a real demonstration of its abilities. It "became more erratic in its movements, making dances in different directions coming back quite close to the cariole and then flitting away. [T]he dogs apparently would not look at it ... when it approached ... closer I could see the hair bristling on their necks."

Just as Little Clerk could barely endure the terror, he felt the glowing apparition begin to move away. When he last saw the terrifying image, it was "no larger than a cat's eye." Moments later it had faded into the northeast night sky and disappeared.

By morning he and his team had gratefully reached the shore. Although the ghost light had not returned, his dogs continued their bizarre behaviour. They were all decidedly anti-social, not the friendly, companionable animals they normally were. Clearly all four had been deeply affected by their experience through the night.

When Little Clerk met with the area magistrate who had come to escort him to the haunted woman, he described his recent encounter with the paranormal. Inevitably, the conversation turned to the purpose of his journey—to investigate the so-called possession. The magistrate had apparently decided that Little Clerk would have to take the woman away with him but when they went to her home, not surprisingly, the woman had fled.

The woman was never found and was presumed to have died shortly after having made her escape. Little Clerk and the magistrate burned her tipi with its medicine bags inside.

Upon reflection, Little Clerk realized that the ghost light, the "foolish fire" that had so frightened him and his dogs, had actually been a manifestation of the haunted woman's spirit.

He closed the article by using a very different writing style than the way in which he began it. Gone was the jaunty, adventuring attitude. No longer was life a challenging escapade to be artfully met by his considerable resources. Clearly, Little Clerk had been visited by a supernatural presence. Clearly, there was much out there in the world that was beyond his understanding and control. In conclusion, he admitted that accompanied lake crossing had been "one of the most uncanny experiences of my long residence in Northwest Canada."

Chapter 6

THE EXPLAINED

Phoney Phantoms

If we believed every report we've ever heard about unidentified flying objects, we'd all be cowering in our basements, hiding from the apparent invasion of aliens. Not all reports of UFO sightings are legitimate or credible—it is that simple. It is equally unreasonable, however, to dismiss all reports of UFOs as swamp gas, especially considering many sightings are over decidedly non-marshy areas.

The same division of "actual" versus "imagined" sightings probably holds true for ghost stories. There is absolutely no doubt in my mind that many people have had legitimate supernatural experiences with spirits, but I also know that, occasionally, what is originally labelled as a ghost story does not hold up to any sort of an investigation. Whatever happened, no matter how seemingly spooky, actually had a very pragmatic explanation.

The following is a collection of just such tales.

With the passage of years the exact site of this "haunted" Winnipeg house has become somewhat confused. We can, however, narrow down the location to approximately the Maryland Street area at some point between the Assiniboine River and George Bell High School.

At the time of this ghost story, the "haunted" house stood in near isolation with "no houses nearer than Furby Street," according to a December 14, 1957, article in the *Winnipeg Free Press.* The house had been deserted for some time and had sunk into a terrible state of disrepair. Windows were broken, shutters hung at precarious angles and banged in the wind, and weeds overgrew the lawn. In short, this house was a place absolutely begging to have at least one spooky story develop around it. And thanks to its location on the periphery of a neighbourhood full of children with fertile imaginations, the dilapidated old place soon had a reputation for being a haunted house.

As luck would have it, both the house's reputation and its foreboding appearance suited its next occupants well—so well that they even went out of their way to encourage gossip about their place being haunted. You see, these were folks who needed their privacy, lots of it. Without complete seclusion, they were not able to carry out their life's work. To guarantee these necessary conditions, the uninvited tenants even promoted stories about angry ghosts in the house.

On one occasion when the occupants observed youngsters from the nearby community venturing onto the property, the men draped themselves in plain white sheets and jumped out threateningly. The startled children didn't bother staying around to hear the special sound effects the "ghosts" had also prepared for them.

Many years later a gentleman identified only as G. Lemieux told his story to the *Free Press*. Lemieux had been a child in the neighbourhood during the "haunted house" era and remembered the old place well. One day after an informal lacrosse game on the fields surrounding the abandoned house, he and one of his friends actually ventured into the house.

The front door was open and, according to Lemieux's reminiscence, he and another lad "apprehensively" made their way inside. Cobwebs and dust greeted the adventurers but, on the first floor at least, not much more than that. Taking courage from the lack of apparent spooks so far, the two proceeded up the staircase to the second floor. If the boys had been judging by outside appearances, it would have been there, on the middle storey, that they should have expected to meet phantoms, for the second storey was considerably spookier-looking, from the outside, than the first floor.

Up the stairs they went, no doubt losing a considerable amount of boyish bravado with each step. The fear that must have crept into their hearts likely diminished their interest in ghost-hunting, but, as with boys everywhere, Lemieux and his buddy were very curious and equally as determined not to lose face in front of their friends.

Cautiously, they made their way through the rooms on the second floor. Perhaps, despite the foreboding appearance of this upper floor, they actually felt reasonably safe up there; the legend they'd heard indicated that the eldest son of the former owner had died from a broken neck after falling down the basement stairs. It was said that the lad's family moved away immediately after the tragedy. The boy's soul remained to haunt the house.

Despite their long-standing familiarity with the undeniably scary story, Lemieux and his friend continued their explorations. After a while they called out an invitation to the less courageous lacrosse players who'd chosen to wait outside. Whether or not the others ever joined the first two that day was not recorded, but the initial exploration served to at least partially debunk the abandoned building's status as a "haunted house."

Most reports of this particular haunted house end here, but Lemieux's retelling included details that provide some most satisfying closure. He recalled many years later, as an adult, making a return visit to Winnipeg from Chicago. During his stay, he chanced upon a "distinguished-looking gentleman with a grey goatee" who "exuded prosperity and well-being." The two began a nostalgic discussion of Winnipeg as it had existed when Lemieux was a lad. Inevitably, the conversation steered itself to the day Lemieux and his friends had ventured into the "haunted house."

The older man inquired as to whether the visitor from Chicago ever knew who owned the house he had described. Lemieux recalled that he'd heard it belonged to a prominent Winnipeg businessman named Hugh Sutherland and that this same Sutherland might have been a direct descendant of the Selkirk settlers as well as being one of the founders of the Canadian Northern Railway.

In reply to that rather detailed description, the older gentleman acknowledged that what Lemieux had been told was correct—for he was Hugh Sutherland and the house had, indeed, belonged to him. As the former owner of the place, Sutherland was able to assure Lemieux that at no time during their trespassing-adventure were any of the boys in any danger of being accosted by a phantom. The house had never been home to a ghost but had been temporarily abandoned while Sutherland fulfilled obligations away from Winnipeg. During this time, a gang of counterfeiters discovered the place and decided that the empty and isolated house was an ideal spot in which to perfect their craft.

The ghost story had developed as a direct result of the criminals' attempts to discourage visitors: "... whenever unwelcome intruders appeared they would cover themselves with sheets outlined with phosphorus and wave their arms to scare them away."

No doubt feeling pleased that his childhood adventure story now had an ending, Lemieux set about getting on with the rest of his life, which included a stint in the army. One evening he and his military tent-mates were telling one another stories to help pass a long and otherwise boring evening. Lemieux's contribution to the evening's recitations was a re-telling of his "ghost" story.

Although he might have had a youth full of adventure stories from which to draw, that evening Lemieux must have been very glad he chose the one he did. As he finished explaining not only the adventure after the lacrosse game but also his coincidental meeting years later with the property's owner, one of his army-mates listening to the tale spoke up.

This second soldier's name was Spence. Lemieux tied this contributor firmly to his Winnipeg heritage by explaining in his 1957 retelling for the *Free Press* that he was a descendant of the person Spence Street was named to honour.

It seems that Spence must have been several years older than Lemieux for when the latter was playing lacrosse and exploring empty houses, Spence was working as a policeman. Not long after Lemieux's adventures in the house, the people in the nearby community asked the police force to look into the old abandoned residence. The concerned citizens suggested that although the place might not be haunted, it was most assuredly home to some very questionable activity.

Accordingly, the police planned a raid on the property. Spence was one of the dozens of officers who hid in the long grasses surrounding the place until the cover of night allowed them to creep closer while remaining unnoticed by whomever or whatever they might discover inside. Over the course of time, the officers reached the entrance to the house, went in and from there split into two groups. As the first bunch headed up the stairs, the second battalion, including Spence, silently made its way into the basement.

It didn't take them long to make out a band of light coming from behind a door frame crudely cut into a basement wall. They knocked on the makeshift door but barged in rather than extending the courtesy of waiting for an answer to their knock. Their raid was an unqualified success. They not only discovered and arrested the "ghosts" who were occupying the property without the owner's consent, but they also discovered and confiscated a well-equipped makeshift mint—"acid, paper, ink and copper plates complete."

With that additional information, we should finally have arrived at the end of a wonderfully convoluted haunted house story. And if human nature was not quite so stubborn (or so fond of ghost stories), the legend would have died with the triumphant police raid. As it was, however, Lemieux assured his readers that despite the overwhelming evidence to the contrary, the house remained "haunted," in the eyes of the community, until the day it was eventually torn down.

In every city or town, there's at least one house that closely resembles everyone's image of what a haunted house should look like. First of all, it should be a large, old house, at least a two-storey, preferably three. Lightning rods on the roof always add to the impression, as do high, deteriorating fences, dark colours, broken shutters flapping in the wind and stands of trees attempting to crowd one another and the house out. Houses that look like this deserve to be haunted. Urban legends are created around these houses.

And this was exactly the case in the following story. Two young men shared the attic suite in a rambling, old place on Alverstone Street. One of the roommates, Pat Romano, eventually became a police officer and one hopes he retained his evident sense of humour while serving on the force.

Initially, the men were somewhat concerned about the "strange sounds [they heard] for a while at night." The scratching did sound eerie—there was no doubt about it—so they decided to investigate on their own. Their efforts were quickly rewarded when they discovered pigeons nesting on the roof of the house and squirrels happily carrying out their daily routines in the walls of the old place.

An exterminator soon put an end to the "ghostly" noises but, of course, could do nothing to change either the appearance or the reputation of the place. Neighbourhood children still ran past the "haunted" house squealing in fearful delight. Rather than try to dissuade the youngsters of their firmly held beliefs, the occupants decided to play into their hands by decorating the already foreboding house in an especially eerie fashion at Halloween. They planted steaming kettles in the many trees on the property and bathed the house with spooky lighting.

As a result, to this day, there are those who will testify that the house on Alverstone Street, which was never occupied by anything more unnatural than squirrels, pigeons and creative tenants, was actually home to a ghost.

The place—Portage La Prairie. The time—mid-July, in the year of our Lord, 1931.

Most people thought tough times had befallen them. What a blessing it was that they did not know then that the toughest of times were still to come. For now, they struggled on as best they could, coping with grain prices that were falling and life-giving rain that was not.

For the moment, however, the people of Portage La Prairie were pre-occupied by a particularly provocative ghost story. Rumours of ghostly sightings had begun days before and by now crowds of men were gathering each evening in an east-end neighbourhood. (According to the write-up that day in the *Evening Tribune*, "... children and many women are taking the nightly appearances very seriously and refuse to go to 'the ghost's' stomping ground unless accompanied by men.")

Presumably there were enough men available to provide escort service, for the numbers of townsfolk gathered was such that the police had to be called "to regulate traffic." By the evening of Wednesday, July 15, the crowd's patience was rewarded for "... the 'ghost' did not disappoint the thrill-seekers. Dressed in long, white robes, he, or she, moved swiftly across the street some eighteen metres ahead of the crowd. There was a gasp of amazement as the 'spirit' made its leisurely way down the street."

For a moment the crowd was still and everyone watched in awe "as the 'spirit' made its way along. Suddenly, one man darted forwards in an attempt to catch the unearthly visitor. The chase was soon taken up by the majority of men in the crowd [thereby leaving the women and children unescorted, it would appear] and a milling throng followed the white-robed figure.

"Mere humans had no chance of catching up. The 'ghost' rapidly outdistanced the crowd and soon [in true ghostly fashion] disappeared on the prairie."

Predictably, the sighting and attempted apprehension caused much excitement throughout the town. "[C]hildren, women and not a few men gathered to discuss the phenomenon. Until long after midnight, little knots of people remained in the vicinity [waiting] for a second appearance, but the show was over for the night."

As folks toddled off to their homes, they made plans to reconvene the following evening. This "ghost" was a mystery they were determined to solve. Everyone had an opinion about what the cause and source of the haunting could possibly be. Some of those convictions were supernatural, others were not. "Police are convinced that some person is playing a practical joke, and they are endeavouring to discover who it is."

In short, Portage La Prairie hadn't had such a collective good time in a while. The fun didn't last very long, however. Just days after the dramatic men-versus-spirit dash down the street, it was discovered that the "ghost" was a young woman attempting to disguise her identity with a white robe for the purpose of a rendezvous with her lover.

Today, the only question that remains about the Depression-era ghost of Portage La Prairie is, given the mores of time and place, what explanation could the parents have offered to their children about the mysterious entity that had briefly injected some excitement into their lives? Odd to think that the community might have found the truth more offensive than the thought that they were sharing their hometown with a phantom.

Both mice and ghosts took turns being blamed for mysterious sounds heard in a bank vault. About 11:00 p.m. on Wednesday, July 28, 1948, cleaners at the Main Street and Lombard Avenue (Winnipeg) branch of the Canadian Bank of Commerce contacted a security guard who in turn called police to report what was described as "tapping" sounds coming from inside the locked safe. Constables and detectives alike converged on the bank and were met there by detectives from the security agency responsible for the branch.

Despite published concerns that the sounds might indicate the bank was haunted, police were inclined to believe that the unusual disturbances came from a more earthbound source. As the vault door was locked with a time-sensitive device, the officers most pressing apprehension was not the possibility of ghosts but rather the possibility that someone very much alive had somehow become trapped in the safe before it had been closed for the night.

Towards this end, detectives contacted workers who had been repairing the bank's security system that day. The men assured police that, although their worries were well founded in that no one could survive in the tiny, airless room overnight, there definitely hadn't been anyone left behind when they put away their tools and left the safe at the end of the day.

As the vault door was set to remain locked until 9:00 a.m. the following morning, police could either verify the workers' information by blowing the door off the vault that night or by waiting until morning to return and open the door the usual way. They decided on the latter course of action and let the night cleaners finish their rounds while entertaining the thought that at any moment they might see an apparition or hear ghostly moans. If any experienced either, the events were not recorded.

Police were back at the branch in the morning in time for the lock to release. They examined the safe carefully and saw that as one slightly disgruntled-sounding officer was heard to mutter, "There's nothing in this vault that shouldn't be here."

What had caused the mysterious tapping sounds then? Eventually, two completely different explanations were offered. The police decided that the ghostly sounds actually came from workers hammering one floor above the bank. The bank's report, however, was much more self-serving. They advised that a newly installed alarm system in the vault would intermittently give off a series of sounds that could be interpreted as a tapping. Further, they were pleased to report that if even those muffled testing sounds alerted security then obviously the new technology was doing its job wonderfully well.

Given the conflicting explanations, maybe it really was a ghost making the sounds after all.

Bibliography

Atwood, Margaret. 1995. *Strange Things*. Oxford: Oxford University Press.

Barton, Winifred G., ed. 1967. *Canada's PSI Century*. Ottawa: The Metaphysical Society of Canada.

Christensen, Jo-Anne. 1996. *Ghost Stories of British Columbia*. Toronto: Hounslow Press.

———. 1995. *Ghost Stories of Saskatchewan*. Toronto: Hounslow Press.

Cleary, Val. 1985. *Ghost Stories of Canada*. Toronto: Hounslow Press.

Colombo, John Robert. 1988. *Mysterious Canada*. Toronto: Doubleday.

Guggenheim, Bill and Judy Guggenheim. 1996. *Hello From Heaven*. New York: Bantam Books.

Ham, George H. 1921. *Reminiscences of a Raconteur*. Winnipeg.

Hervey, Sheila. 1973. *Some Canadian Ghosts*. Richmond Hill: Pocket Books.

Knight, Stephen. 1984. *The Brotherhood, The Secret World of the Freemasons*: New York: Stein and Day.

Phoenix: The Journal of the Unexplained, August/September 1996. Issue 4. East Sussex, United Kingdom.

Phoenix: The Journal of the Unexplained, October/November 1996. Issue 5. East Sussex, United Kingdom.

Rutkowski, Chris. 1993. *Unnatural History, True Manitoba Mysteries*. Winnipeg: Chameleon Publishers.

Smith, Barbara. 1993. *Ghost Stories of Alberta*. Toronto: Hounslow Press.

Sonin, Eileen. 1970. *More Canadian Ghosts*. Richmond Hill: Pocket Books.

Newspaper Stories

The Albertan, January 25, 1934.

The Chronicle, October 21, 1920.

The Daily Free Press, February 21, 1878.

The Edmonton Journal, June 1, 1909.

Manitoba Free Press, October 23, 1905; October 25, 1905.

News of the North, February 12, 1964.

Winnipeg Evening Tribune, July 16, 1931.

Winnipeg Free Press: October 27, 1992; October 22, 1982; October 30, 1982; October 31, 1980; November 24, 1978; October 22, 1977; October 30, 1965; January 18, 1958; December 14, 1957; June 25, 1955; January 5, 1952; August 1, 1952; July 29, 1949; August 12, 1938; August 23, 1938; December 11, 1913; December 7, 1896; March 17, 1898.

Winnipeg Sun, April 5, 1992.